GW01246642

Zen and the Diary of
a B&B Owner

by

Scott Barfield

**Grosvenor House
Publishing Limited**

This book is published by
Grosvenor House Publishing Ltd
28-30 High Street, Guildford, Surrey, GU1 3HY.
www.grosvenorhousepublishing.co.uk

A CIP record for this book
is available from the British Library

ISBN 978-1-907211-07-2

For Helen, who has been with me every step of the way.

Chapters

Introduction   **1**

November - Please could I have a fork?   5

December - "London crew" to break my legs?   27

January - BBC types and leather bondage?   49

February - Allo, I am French.   73

March - "Axe-wielding, medicated, psycho nutter."   93

April - Launderette irony.   121

May - Hemmeroid-injected meat?   145

June - Wedding night threesome?   171

July - Lesbians and tomatoes.   195

August - Are you a "Catty" or a "Protty?"   211

September - Don't mention the Hitler.   233

October - Oh yes, the national star.   253

November Again - A full year!   275

Epilogue   **281**

Introduction

Ever thought about leaving your job to run a B&B? Bored of the same routine and want to ditch it all for a new exciting life being your own boss? Read on if you have because, after doing it myself for the last year, there are plenty of stories which you may find quite interesting. Or maybe that should be rephrased to quite 'unbelievable' or even 'horrifying.'

I kid you not, there are things that happen when running a B&B that you have definitely not considered before or even thought humanly possible. When fantasising about leaving behind the stultifying office job and 'pain in the backside' boss, you have glamorised undoubtedly an alternative existence that may not entirely be grounded in reality.

Have you ever contemplated, for instance, getting stuck in the middle (not literally though) between a twenty-two stone homophobic Afrikaner who objects strongly to naked gay men who lock themselves out of their room in the middle of the night? Or perhaps it has never crossed your mind that drunk Belgian guests can somehow mistake a sink for a toilet (yes, think the worst?) Or that the police may have to help you remove a gangster *wannabe* who is threatening to get his 'London crew down to break your legs?' You also have possibly not considered before that you could answer the door at 3am in the morning to a woman squatting in the street urinating who excuses herself because she is 'desperate for a wee' but wants to know whether you have the phone number of the B&B next door because she has lost her key?

It's not all bad experiences however (honest!) The interesting people do far outnumber the nightmare ones - when film directors stay after giving public talks at the university or an actor performing at the local theatre gives you free tickets. Life can also be a lot duller than a well known music producer staying along with an Asian pop superstar recording his latest album.

Furthermore you are constantly surprised and amused by the numerous situations and experiences which continually keep happening without prediction. The Japanese guests that want to take digital pictures from every angle of 'the British Breakfast.' The German guy that exclaims loudly in the breakfast room 'please could I have a fuck (instead of fork)?' Or the middle aged couples who only check-in for a few hours to fulfil a 'naughty few hours by the sea' fantasy.

There is also the advantage, of course, in buying a B&B (or at least one which is in Brighton) that you get to live by the sea yourself and in the middle of all the things that people come and stay with you to enjoy. And for those of you who are not familiar with Brighton it is renowned supposedly as the one of the bohemian centres of the country where every other person is an artist, musician or media trendy (or at least there are enough people here who go around proclaiming their own trendiness). Henceforth probably the much used tag of Brighton being 'London-by-the-Sea.'

This may or may not portray the true cosmopolitan reality of the city but allows a fair assertion, at least, that culture here shows a degree of evolution compared to some of our other beloved coastal resorts. And given the popularity of Brighton I am sure it will be of great interest to many of you reading this book. Indeed, with eight million visitors a year to Brighton, there is a chance even that some of you may have actually stayed in this very establishment. How interesting this could be then? Not only do you get the inside story of the life of a B&B owner but also you could be one of the stars of the show yourself!

Why the Zen? There are two main reasons for this. Firstly, of course, are all of you lot. When you share your house with three to four thousand strangers a year it is inevitable that your horizons are broadened far more than if you're stuck in the same office every day with the same people having the same conversation about the weather. Inasmuch then as Zen signifies a path towards gaining Truth and Knowledge then who better to learn from than the collective wisdom of the general public (well, carefully selected guests for a B&B experiment anyway?) Secondly, and I must confess at the outset that conceivably this could be slightly self-indulgent, is my own wisdom. Now I don't want to set myself up as some sort of cult leader, although I have heard starting your own religion can be a good way to riches, but some of us are able to enlighten for others the path to Knowledge. Ok, I admit it, the truth is really that in my previous life before running a B&B I was an academic and because that never quite worked out I'm now left solely with the pretence of being an amateur philosopher.

So, if you have any interest at all in the actual realities of leaving your job to run a B&B, or just want to discover some insightful knowledge about the human condition through the prism of an ex-academic sharing his house with a bunch of strangers, then continue with pleasure. Please do not be too offended though if you read on and recognize yourself in any of these pages. Surely, after all, it must be the prerogative of a B&B owner to recount stories of guests however they see fit?

NOVEMBER

Please could I have a fork?

Wednesday 10th November

What have I done? Sitting in the basement of a B&B in central Brighton with seven letting bedrooms upstairs, two of which are occupied before I have even set foot in the front door.

Now I guess one should really have a sense of exhilaration with adrenaline and pride in the new life to be. However, the truth is that I merely feel tired, stressed and full of apprehension. All my worldly possessions lay scattered around in unopened boxes and it is late as the last of them are carried from the self-drive lorry wedged haphazardly on the street outside.

My anxiety is also not helped particularly by the last words of advice from my dad as he set off home after helping me unload.

'Rather you than me to be honest … It's not really the ideal place for Helen to be living and working either is it? If I were you I would make sure you keep a baseball bat or something handy in case there is any trouble … Anyway all the best and hope it works it out.'

Yes. Cheers for that encouragement. I feel much better. Almost as uplifting as the last conversation I had with my mum.

'I know it's what you have chosen to do but I just worry whether you have made the right decision? I mean are you *absolutely* sure that there is not something better you could do with your education?'

Fair enough. Parents only want the best for their kids and maybe it is a rather strange 'career' decision.

However, there are plenty of other people in the world who have gone down the same road. Why not look on the bright side instead? I'm fortunate enough to have a house in the first place that can be traded up for a B&B in Brighton. Or the fact that I don't have to spend the next few years struggling to find a short term temporary contract in academia. Perhaps, even, I'll never have to use a baseball bat in my own house and instead meet lots of fascinating people who will give me great material to write a book?

Thursday 11th November

Luckily on our first ever breakfast only two guests came down to be served which allowed us enough flexibility to run through with ease the routine laid out in detail and pinned on the fridge door by the previous owner. Slightly strange maybe for the guests, seeing a bewildered looking couple that had a rather drastic metamorphose overnight, but they kindly seemed rather excited about the transformation and the honour of being our guinea pigs (I mean first paying customers).

Aside from the sleepless night worrying about what I had committed to and getting used to the unfamiliar scenario of strangers sharing your front door and house, there are also the normal stresses involved with moving. I'd always thought previously that it was somewhat incongruous that the three biggest stresses you encounter supposedly in life are bereavement, divorce and moving house. Surely a close family member or your partner dying is bit more troublesome than exchanging one home for another? However, after spending hours connecting up electrical equipment and fruitlessly trying to arrange new utility accounts and a functioning telephone, it all suddenly appeared perfectly clear why the forces of inertia are so great for any sensible person. Why subject yourself to thousands of unforeseen irritants and months of legal and financial wrangling? Still not quite in the same league as bereavement really is it?

Friday 12th November

A good feeling of exhilaration today surprisingly. Could possibly have something to do with being full last night, which posed no problems, and a wallet now that seems to be bulging unfamiliarly with cash. Gaining such avaricious pleasure from business would no doubt horrify the romantic artistic delusions of my younger self. Isn't there a saying though that states 'only those without a heart don't believe in socialism when they are young and only those without a head don't believe in capitalism when they're older.' Perhaps it's true? Or is it only true for the older ones who are actually making money? Either way any previous young philosophic outlook such as 'the road of excess leads to the palace of wisdom' or 'no eternal reward will forgive us now for wasting the dawn' all seem a bit sanctimonious now. I've found my new palace and the reward for the moment is £350 cash.

Saturday 13th November

It's probably not unexpected that the former owners failed to mention the electrical fire which apparently took place earlier in the year. A French guy staying, however, who is a regular, soon informed us about the fire and the near loss of his 'precious clothes' collection. Michel is about forty years old and runs a rock music bar in the South of France but visits Brighton often 'to go shopping.' Michel's well tended long hair, masses of jewellery and slightly camp nature also make him distinctively on the 'glam' side of being a rocker.

'I'm a bit of a girl when it comes to shopping. If I see something nice I just have to have it. That's why I bought this £500 leather jacket. Next time I come to Brighton I'm going to treat myself to a new tattoo.'

Apparently when the fire broke out the B&B had to be evacuated in the middle of the night.

'Smoke was pouring out of one of the windows but I guessed the fire was not too serious and rushed back in to bring all my clothes out. I didn't care that the firemen were shouting at me. My clothes collection is not like the average persons. It is very expensive and would be very hard to find again and replace.'

Although feeling distinctly dowdy whilst standing next to Michel, at least my everyday collection of high street jeans and t-shirts means my life will never have to be risked in any future fire outbreak.

Sunday 14th November

I wasn't quite expecting, in having the first lengthy conversations with a guest, to eventually discover them to be a fascist activist. Tom, a single man in his mid-fifties, checked in yesterday with stories galore of a past that included working with the Israeli security forces to being a professional rugby player in Australia.

'Been travelling for forty years. I've seen it all. Sixties, seventies, eighties, nineties.'

Tom's a big guy who looks like a bouncer and has also worked as a doorman 'all around the world.'

'Made plenty of money getting people to stick a tenner in to guess my weight. Always think I'm sixteen/seventeen stone and then get on the scales and I'm twenty-one/twenty-two stone.'

At breakfast this morning, very keen to talk politics, Tom bemoaned today's society to me in long meandering rants.

'...people don't look at you in the street anymore or talk ... Men don't have anywhere to go now either to let off steam ... In my day all the men would go down the local pub on a Sunday and talk while the women cooked a roast ... They've even abolished two separate bars in most pubs these days so men can't be themselves and talk freely ... It's political correctness that has done it. Ruined things.'

Although I did try and puncture Tom's conservative mourning of lost 'good old days' with an ironic quip about every previous generation having the advantage of fighting a war to help foster a sense of community, he actually agreed strongly with that proposition before starting another fulmination about bringing back national service. The rant ended when Tom commented on a perfectly pleasant couple who had left the dining room, no doubt glad to escape his moaning.

'Probably has gypsy blood in her that one. Nice couple though I guess. Just can tell a bit of rough.'

Monday 15th November

Tom nabbed me once more for some bizarre meandering statements.

'I know all the pubs in London where the political crowd hang out. New Labour are always in the Red Lion and all of them, from every party, are big boozers before getting their trains back to the constituencies. Tony Blair is gay. Everyone in London knows he had an affair with 'Mandy' [Peter Mandelson]. That's why Blair gave him that cushy job in Europe on the EU gravy train.'

'I do go to the gay pubs myself when I'm here in Brighton,' Tom continued uninterrupted. 'I'm not gay or anything. I like the music they play. I can go into a gay bar as well without people staring at me thinking I'm either the old bill or a gangster. I'm not gay though myself of course.'

At this stage I was slightly baffled in making out who Tom was exactly? Conservative, sexist thug who could potentially get aggressive if you disagreed with him? Seemingly intelligent guy who cared deeply about community? Tabloid fantasist? Closet homosexual? It was then that he casually dropped another revelation into the conversation.

'I'm a member of the British National Party you know. An activist for Nick Griffin [the BNP's leader]. I've nothing against Asians/Blacks though so long as they're born here. Just think there should be no new arrivals and we should concentrate on our own. I'm not into bashing anyone or anything like that. That's the National Front lot not the BNP. I'd leave if it was, especially if it got to guns and stuff being used.'

At this point I decided to stop the ironic quips to keep the conversation going – didn't want to explore any further the relative merits of 'guns and stuff' politics.

Tuesday 16th November

Helen and I went for a walk today along the pier which is an obligatory part of any visit to Brighton even if the attraction, with its amusements and Victorian facade, appears somewhat outdated in the twenty-first century. We noticed a couple ahead who were guests of ours and saw that they realised we were walking towards them. As we approached, however, they deliberately avoided eye contact and pretended to have not seen us. Maybe Tom is right about people these days! Although I suspect it was more just a case of English shyness where a large number of people are petrified of any social interaction. Alternatively, of course, they merely thought we were boring pains in the neck and couldn't be bothered to waste their time with us?

Wednesday 17th November

Could it have been a Freudian slip? Karl, a single German male guest, at breakfast this morning, gesticulated over to me that he had a problem by holding up a knife. Apparently the table had not been fully laid out properly and a fork was missing from the place setting. Karl's heavy accent, however, spoken slowly and loudly, resulted in the whole dining room hearing him announce wrongly the problem with his cutlery.

'Excuse me, Scott. Please could I have a fuck?'

If alone, the mispronunciation would probably have passed without comment. However, as the entire dining room erupted into giggles it was a bit hard to ignore.

'I'm sorry Karl but you will have to pay extra for that kind of service. And not during breakfast either,' I replied as two other German female guests explained to Karl in their native tongue why everyone was laughing. Still, I did kindly take him over a fork afterwards to finish his breakfast.

Thursday 18th November

We saw the live show of *The League of Gentleman* at the Brighton Centre last night. Sitting a few rows in front of us was Norman Cook, a.k.a. local superstar DJ 'Fatboy Slim.' As I pointed him out to Helen I could see quite a few others doing exactly the same thing and staring over. It must be quite unnerving to be famous - surely it would be hard to not be extremely self-conscious all the time and irritated by the weight of people's whispering and gawping. Still, I did glance over a few more times myself just to check whether Norman was enjoying the show or not - in fact, I probably helped to spoil it for him.

Friday 19th November

'Goodness gracious, I've had much cheaper quotes from other B&B's,' a woman exclaimed indignantly today on the phone after asking for our room prices. 'Well if that's how much you charge I'll be staying elsewhere,' she added before abruptly hanging up.

Good. Go elsewhere then. And why not apply the same flawed logic to the rest of your life? Walk into a salubrious wine bar and exclaim out loud, 'Blimey, £16 for a bottle of wine. No, thank you. I can get pissed much cheaper on a bottle of meths down the local park.' Or go into a BMW car showroom and tell them how scandalous their prices are when you 'can get a second-hand *Trebant* for a fraction of the cost.'

Saturday 20th November

Surely there is no need for women to be embarrassed about owning a vibrator in these enlightened days?

'Sorry I don't know where that buzzing noise is coming from,' I said today when showing two young women into a twin room.

After a few minutes of searching the room, checking the electrics and appliances, the source of the repetitive buzzing noise was still a mystery. Then I suddenly realised the sound was coming from inside one of the suitcases.

'Oh, that's good. At least there is nothing wrong with the room,' I said.

'It's just my "massage" hairbrush making the noise, honest,' was the quick reply by one of the women accompanied by a mortified expression.

Although my initial thoughts had been a mobile phone buzzing in the suitcase, the flustered reaction immediately turned the imagery into a vibrator that had switched itself on. As all three of us stood there

awkwardly I probably did not help to defuse the embarrassment.

'Well, you better turn it off quick, otherwise the
batteries will run out,' I said smiling.

Sunday 21st November

We have had another French guest staying for the last
couple of nights with his girlfriend. He is in his late
forties with shoulder length hair and the manner somewhat of an ageing hippy, albeit in a distinct Gallic style
with a fusion of intellectual sincerity and pretentious-
ness. As the couple checked out this morning our French
friend noticed the guitar in our lounge which induced a
lengthy (mainly monologue) conversation about his
'wonderful love' for music.

'Ah, I see you play the guitar. It is a beautiful instru-
ment. I also play. I like all styles from classical, folk,
jazz, rock and even pop as well. Music is such a wonderful thing. It can truly take you to places far away. I'm
a big fan of world music also and I have travelled a lot,
especially around South America. Listening to music
not only can take you literally back to these places but
there is something else, a different level of shared con-
sciousness that it brings on. It is almost like an out of
body experience when you listen sometimes. It can be
truly beautiful.'

'Yes, I do enjoy music but you probably wouldn't
want to listen to me playing the guitar.' I said with a self-
deprecating laugh.

'Ah, I'm sure you are an expert. In fact we have just
been to see some gigs in Brighton whilst here. I really find

the music scene here so vibrant and maybe go to a couple of different gigs a night. I've probably come to Brighton over fifty times now mainly just to see live music. I'm always over here. It's my passion to hear music. In my flat in Paris I have over three thousand records that "live" with me in the front room. I have been collecting for nearly forty years now and all of these records are a part of me. They each have a story, a meaning and a place in my life that is special. All of my records have such a distinct memory and a feeling for me.'

'Well it's good to have such a passion for something in life. And how did you want to pay the bill - with cash or by credit card?'

'Ah, and I see you have many books as well. They are such a wonderful gift in life also. To stimulate the mind and open up the world. I have many books in my flat too...'

At this point our French friend started to scan the bookshelf (which is just near the reception desk near the door) with further long monologues of equal flowery pontificating on his 'love' of books. Eventually the bill was settled, however, and he shook my hand goodbye.

'I wish you both a beautiful and full life.'

Monday 22 nd November

A Portuguese man was due to arrive into Gatwick this evening from Lisbon and check-in with us around 8pm. Our guest, looking like a Portuguese version of Leo Sayer, with his black hair sporting an impressive 1970's perm, finally turned up three and a half hours later than expected.

'I am very sorry,' he immediately said in slow, heavily-accented English. 'I am late because my *spaceship* got delayed.'

Now unless there is some form of extra-terrestrial transport, only open to all Leo Sayer lookalikes that I am not yet aware of, something may have got lost here in translation.

Tuesday 23rd November

Unfortunately, in relation to the male species, a level of discrimination seems to be the wise choice - especially when dealing with single men. A number of times already now we have had single men looking for a 'cheap room' who have made us feel extremely uncomfortable on our own doorstep. A guest we were not sure about last night, but let in anyhow, has reinforced perhaps why we have been right to turn people away.

Maybe it is a bit unfair to falsely say that you are fully booked but it certainly saves you the ongoing stress of having a stranger in your house that you do not trust. It also prevents unpleasant discoveries, as we found this morning in the room let last night, where all four pillows had been laid systematically out on the bed with a fresh deposit of sperm on each of them. Is that socially acceptable behaviour? I think not.

Now we can understand that people have some basic needs and have no intention of putting up signs prohibiting masturbation, but apply tissues, not the ritualised use of our pillows which we have to strip and clean. And what is the psychology of a man who deliberately whacks off onto pillows *wanting* someone else to find it?

Strikes me as being at least one rung on the ladder of a sex offender, which is not a ladder I want anywhere near my house. Perhaps my dad was right after all about that baseball bat?

Wednesday 24th November

Was it a bad idea to place lilies on the dining room window sill close to one of the guest tables? Lilies, of course, are attractive flowers but there is the downside of being badly stained if brushed with the pollen which ruined one of my shirts last week. A guest today, however, not only managed to get pollen stains down his jacket but also all over the back of his hair. The elderly gentleman had obviously shifted his chair too far back during breakfast despite being prior warned 'to be careful of the pollen.' I only noticed the stains as the couple left the dining room and (shamefully?) kept quiet as nothing but a polite 'thank you' was said on departure. Perhaps red Mohicans will become a new trendy fashion statement for old men?

Thursday 25th November

I've often heard that working with the general public can be a 'nightmare' and booking Mr Porter in over the telephone perhaps encapsulates why this maxim is true - a certain percentage of people are just immensely annoying. Below is an edited version of a longer conversation that eventually led to the reservation being cancelled from sheer exasperation.

'I have a booking in three weeks time to watch the speedway and I'll be arriving early about 9am in the morning and want to know what time I can collect my key.'

'Well check-in time on Sunday is 12pm but you are welcome to arrive earlier and leave your bags with us until the room is ready.'

'Mmm, not sure about that really. What do you mean I can leave my bags? Where will they be and how will I get my key?'

'We have a secure place you can store your luggage and you will be able to come back and collect the key to your room anytime after 12pm.'

'I don't like the sound of this. How can I be sure that I will get my key? What happens if I come back later and can't get access to my bags? Why can't I just have my key in the morning?'

'Well check-out time for other guests is not until 11am and then obviously we need a certain amount of time to change and clean the room. We're offering to store your luggage as an extra favour before our usual check-in times begin.'

'I'm really not sure about this. I'm going off to watch the speedway and I want to leave my bags in my room. I don't trust that they will be safe anyway else and how can I be sure that I will be able to collect my key later?'

'I tell you what Mr Porter. As you're clearly so concerned about your stay with us. I'm going to cancel the booking and thus relieve you of the stress that we are evidently causing you.'

'Yes but I'm coming to Brighton to watch the speedway and I'm going to need somewhere to stay.'

'I'm sure you will be able to find somewhere else easily. Thank you and goodbye.'

Friday 26th November

An event happened for the first time this morning which, in retrospect, is probably a common occurrence in hotels/B&Bs but not something you would necessarily consider in advance as a potential embarrassing hazard of the job. As usual, before going in to service one of the rooms, a knock was made to check that the occupants were out for the day. There was no answer or noise so I entered the room and started to tidy and straighten up whilst humming merrily to myself. After about a minute, though, of being in the room, I suddenly become aware that in the en suite bathroom there was a person on the toilet who was nervously trying to alert me to their presence by coughing in a deliberate fashion. As this person had not locked the en suite door (and was obviously too shy to shout out directly whilst sitting on the toilet) it was lucky they decided to pursue the 'coughing strategy' because the bathroom was about to be tidied up next. That, of course, could have been more embarrassing for both of us and, as I quietly left the room to leave the guest in peace, I made a note to always check in the future that the bathrooms are empty first. In this particular case, however, had I actually left the room a bit too quietly thereby leaving the guest in suspended angst as to whether someone was still there or not? Would it have been best to go back in and tell them not to worry?

Saturday 27th November

Listening to Radio Four at breakfast this morning we were delighted by a segment which came on outlining the details of a man who actively seeks out fresh 'road kill' as a source of food (free, good sustenance, and environmentally beneficial, apparently.)

'Oh great,' I said to Helen. 'Do you think we should go and switch over the station out there [in the dining room]?'

Just as I walked out to where the guests were contentedly eating their breakfast, a middle aged woman, sitting with her husband, suddenly sat up bolt straight with a look of horror across her face.

'My goodness. They're talking about eating road kill,' she exclaimed out loud.

'I'm really sorry,' I quickly jumped in, 'Would you like me to change the radio station for you?'

'No. No. It's alright,' she replied but still with a look of astonishment. 'I just really can't believe that anybody could possibly do such a thing.'

I was going to make a joke and reassure her that all our meat is freshly sourced, 'from the butchers not the road,' but judged her to be too sensitive - did not want to create any more doubt as she ate our bacon and sausages.

Sunday 28th November

'I am from Canada and will be vacationing in the UK next month. I have seen your B&B on the internet as a potential place to stay but would first like to clarify some points; (1) I suffer from a lot of allergies so need to know whether your house is clean? (2) Because of my allergies I would also like to know more about your cleaning products - do you use natural chemicals? (3) I am very sensitive to dust - do you have carpets or floorboards in your house?'

Sensing this potential guest could be an obsessive compulsive nut - visions of *Wacko Jacko* style face masks and further requests to sleep in an oxygen capsule (which we do not provide) - I decided to reply only with our standard email response listing prices. However, this did not deter the woman, and today she phoned up:

'Hello. I did send an email recently requesting some information but did not get any answers. Could I ask some questions now please?'

'Certainly. What would you like to know?'

'I suffer from a lot of allergies and am very sensitive to dirt and dust. Is your B&B kept in a clean state?'

'Of course,' I said whilst really wanting to say, 'Well, it's ok I guess. Bit of cat shit here and there but otherwise it's fine.'

'So cleanliness is a high standard then? It's just that I've stayed in other places that supposedly have a good reputation and they haven't been very clean. There isn't any mould in the bathrooms is there?'

After another few questions along the same lines, and me biting my tongue with polite answers, the woman actually went ahead and booked the room. Damn. Five minutes later, though, she phoned back:

'I've just made a reservation with you but would like to cancel please. I'm just not sure still about the cleanliness and do not want to take any risks.'

Normally a cancellation is a bit of a disappointment but this one was made gladly.

Monday 29th November

Cleaning a room today after a middle aged woman had checked out and we found two teabags *inside* the kettle, which was also stained indelibly with brown marks. Is it normal to use a kettle as a teapot?

Tuesday 30th November

Have you heard the one about a naked gay guy and a twenty-two stone homophobic Afrikaner? No me neither until now - and not a scenario I ever expected to encounter actually.

At 2am last night I awoke to hear a repetitive knocking noise from somewhere but soon drifted back to sleep. At 2.45am I was awoken again. This time the sound was louder and definitely coming from inside the house and I could hear someone shouting and banging on a door.

As I go up the stairs, in my dressing gown, I am confronted by a male guest standing stark naked on the first floor landing.

'Let me in Gary. This is not funny. Let me in. Open the door. Do you hear me? Let me in. The joke has gone too far.'

'What's going on? And do you want to keep the noise down please or you'll wake the whole house.'

'I was just using the toilet on the stairs but unfortunately got locked out of my room and can't wake my partner.'

'You could have rang our bell you know and we would have let you back in. And why are you naked in the corridor anyway?'

'Well naked or not I should not have to put up with homophobic abuse. And you should be ashamed of yourself for letting such people stay. It is not acceptable. All gays should be dead is what he said to me. And threatened also to punch my head in. You should call the police. In fact I want the police called right now,' was the unexpected response, whilst standing in front of me with all bits still dangling.

The door then opened to the room adjacent and out stepped a 6ft 5inch Afrikaner with a big goatee beard and probably a lot of muscle with the fat.

'My girlfriend and me found this idiot about an hour ago laying naked curled up on the floor. Since then he has been banging on the door whilst we are trying to get to sleep. That's what's been happening here.'

'And you think that gives you the right to be homo-phobic does it? And threaten me with violence? The police should be called and have him arrested.'

'Do I really have to put up with this? A naked imbe-cile in front of my girlfriend, outside our room, stopping us getting to sleep?'

At this point I decided it was best to try and defuse the situation and let everyone calm down. And not least also because I'm getting fed up myself with naked gesticulating and bits bouncing around in the process.

'Look. The police are not going to be called. I'm going to let you back into your room [by some minor miracle, or more likely a deliberate ruse, "Gary" had still not woken up and opened the door] and there will be no more naked trips to the bathroom again. This gentleman and his girlfriend are then going to get some sleep and will not bother or threaten you anymore. Ok?'

The Afrikaner couple were at breakfast this morning but thankfully the other two did not show up, so an awkward atmosphere or repeat confrontation was avoided.

'Yeh, I did tell him to shut up and where to go but the idiot was really pissing me off. Honestly, I couldn't believe it. He just steamed straight towards me as well. A naked gay guy running towards me at my bedroom door at 2am in the morning. Unbelievable. If I was back in South Africa I would have taken the bastard out completely. He was after my cock, I tell you. That's all they think about.'

Another interesting episode and story to tell. But is this new life fun?

DECEMBER

"London crew" to break my legs?

Wednesday 1ˢᵗ December

As a man, could the ageing process be an even more deflating experience than normal, if you have previously spent large amounts of your time wearing heavy make-up and dressed in women's clothing?

'I'm a drag queen you know. I was performing last night but I'm enjoying myself so much that I'm going to need to stay in town for another night,' an extremely camp man, a bit tipsy, announced when knocking on the door today.

'Oh you should have seen my show. How beautiful I looked. So glamorous and pretty. I was hot stuff, darling. The audience just adored me.'

The exuberance then continued as the man pouted and re-performed some of his act on the way up to the room. However, when confronted by the enormous ornamental mirror on our first-floor landing, the high-spirits abruptly ended. Our drag artist friend, standing suddenly still and quiet, stared glumly at his middle aged reflection and receding hairline.

'Oh dear. So beautiful last night. So much nicer than the male version of me.'

Thursday 2ⁿᵈ December

Fittingly for a city that still has a hedonistic reputation is the history behind the Royal Pavilion building, which is one of Brighton's premier tourist attractions. The Prince

Regent, who later became King George IV, apparently built the 'exotic' palace as a discreet hideaway for liaisons with his frowned upon lover (she was Catholic) and because seawater was recommended as beneficial for his gout (disease of opulent lifestyles).

Most tourists are impressed by the history and unique architecture of the palace, which is impossible to miss on the main road as you enter the city. Some American guests staying with us, however, were confused as to whether they had actually seen the 'real' Pavilion or not?

'Is that building just round the corner, the one that's lit up at night with the funny round towers, actually the Royal Pavilion or is it just a small replica hotel?'

'Yes. That's the one. The real thing.'

'Wow. It's so small. We thought it would be much bigger.'

'Well, they've probably got one in Las Vegas that is bigger.'

'Yes they might have I guess. There are certainly lots of replica buildings there.'

Friday 3rd December

Some guests today were telling their friends about an amusing travel documentary they had seen on TV a few nights before. I had actually seen the same programme so was even more amused to share in their laughter as I over-heard the story being relayed. The TV presenter was at a market stall in Indonesia which sold fresh eggs from a number of live hens being kept. The Indonesian family were telling the presenter about their livelihood and showing him a hen which was about to lay an egg. As the bird was held up to the presenter he felt obliged to follow their instruction to 'insert his finger' to see if an egg was about to be delivered - the same method which they use. After ten to fifteen seconds of his finger being inserted into the female hen, and wiggling it around to try and 'feel for the egg,' the Indonesian family all suddenly fell about laughing. Not really a method they use, just a practical joke! I don't know whether this is typical Indonesian humour, or not, but it made me and lots of the guests laugh - even whilst eating eggs for breakfast at the same time. I think even the hen had a smile on her face.

Saturday 4th December

It's great when the dining room is mixed with French and English couples and a bit of cross-cultural exchange can occur.

'Cor my heads banging. I was so pissed last night,' an English guy said out loud as he came down for breakfast.

'Really good night though. Really good night. You lot [to the blankly staring French couples] should try out Wetherspoons. It's open until 1am in the morning and cheap so you can get right off your rocker without breaking the bank.'

Sunday 5th December

Our English guest from yesterday had previously asked me to recommend a good Chinese restaurant because it was his girlfriend's favourite and he wanted a nice birthday surprise for her.

'Aahh, we had an absolutely corking meal last night.'

'Oh did you find the Chinese restaurant I told you about?'

'Oh no. We went to Aberdeen Steak House. Superb steak. Steak Diane sauce. Fantastic. Never had that sauce before - have you ever heard of it?'

Later on I bumped into him again, without his girl-friend, and he was carrying a naff looking bunch of plastic flowers.

'I just got these as an extra present for the girl. Dirt cheap from the pound shop but she'll be happy with them.'

Monday 6th December

What explains precisely the psychology behind some people's behaviour when confronted with 'eat-as-much-as-you-like' food? Surely it's not normal or desirable for one person to eat a large bowl of cereal, yoghurt, banana and apple, full English breakfast with a rack of toast, two croissants, an extra couple of toast rounds with jams/marmalade, finished off with an orange and some plums - all scoffed down in the space of twenty five minutes just after getting up? Which is the greater moti-vator - pure gluttony or miserliness? No doubt there are recess genes in all of us which makes us want to feast when given the chance to counteract any potential famine round the corner. Likewise, if something is being offered for free (literally on a plate in this case), then there might be some evolutionary logic to take as much as possible. But have we not evolved a bit now? Gorging on so much food that you feel sick all day and are hardly able to walk back up the stairs can't be a rationally sensible choice, whether on holiday or not? And just because it's already included in the price, it must really be false economy to stuff your face so much to solely try and save a few pence later in the day. A bit of honesty though to counteract sounding too sanctimonious, the truth is I'm the exact type of person that does overindulge in such situations - nothing to do with money in my case, just greed.

Tuesday 7th December

If a German guest shows an authoritarian concern about a general lack of efficiency and the right-thinking of others then, obviously, you have no choice but to humour them.

'We must change the way the [former] East Germans think. They are too lazy after communism. We must make their minds think differently and they will be more productive. That is why the unemployment is so high in the East and the economy so poor.'

'How do you think their minds can be changed to make them more efficient?'

'This is the problem. They have been used to not working hard for so long that it is difficult for them to change. It is very hard to make them see the world *properly*.'

Could be a valid point? Communism with its job security and zero unemployment, coupled with relative egalitarianism probably does give a distorted view of reality. How can people be made though to appreciate that the 'real' world is all about job insecurity and inequality and being as economically efficient as possible?

Wednesday 8th December

Elderly women – the lengths they go to these days for their thrills! At 4.30am this morning we both get woken up by the loud clanging of a fire alarm going off. Initially, believing it to be our own alarm, we jumped out of bed in a panic only to then realise shortly after that the noise was actually coming from next door. Following a quick check to make sure there was no real problem we retired back to bed and waited for the clanging to stop.

Later in the day our neighbours informed us that they suspected a stranger had been brought back by one of their guests and, after some altercation, had decided to smash the fire alarm glass on leaving the premises. The whole house had been evacuated as the fire brigade made sure it was a false alarm. One young guy, who had been staying in a room on the top floor, reacted so quickly in panic that he was left standing outside wearing only a jacket that barely covered his bum and private parts. Our neighbour, more preoccupied by organising the fire drill, had not noticed this semi-naked gentleman until two elderly women guests had cheerily pointed it out to her.

'It was probably these elderly women that smashed the alarm!' I told my neighbour. 'Keep a close eye on those women tonight, especially if the same "young man" is still staying.'

Thursday 9th December

Typical Brighton *luvvie* types stopped in front of me in the 'Lanes' shopping area today.

'How are you, darling? Oh you look fabulous. I saw you on TV last night. You were good. Very good.'

'Ooh, thank you, darling. You're so kind. I have to say it has been a blast. An absolute blast. You think I came across well then?'

'Oh yes. Fabulous. Fabulous.'

Friday 10th December

Oh no! Not another example of that baseball bat being needed. About 10.30pm we heard a brief bit of shouting at the back of the house but, not sure where it was coming from, just ignored it. Our neighbours, about ten minutes later, knocked on the door.

'Sorry to disturb you but guests of yours have been having a big argument with each other from the room on the second floor. When the man saw us looking up from the terrace he started hurling abuse in our direction as well and also threw this directly at us [the bin from the communal toilet on our stairway landing].'

When I went upstairs to investigate there were no other guests in apart from the room which our neighbours had alleged the shouting and bin had been thrown from. The guy in the room was a Cockney in his late-thirties with a shaved head and an attitude. The arguing at least appeared to have halted though because all was quiet when I knocked on the door.

'We've had a complaint from our neighbours about shouting from this room and objects being thrown at their terrace. Do you know anything about this?'

'What you going on about geezer? Don't know what you're talking about.'

'Look. We have two quiet older couples in the other two back bedrooms, both of whom are not in at the moment. This [the bin] is from that toilet. We know you have just been having an argument so do you want to give me any explanation as to how this landed on our neighbours' terrace?'

'Nothing to fucking do with me mate so leave me and my girlfriend alone will yer. In fact, if you're gonna disturb us like this we're gonna want some fucking compensation from yer.'

Helen, who had now joined me on the landing, retorted to this request with a grunt to suggest 'you must be joking.'

'And I dunno what you're fucking laughing about Ginger.'

'We don't have to put up with abusive behaviour in our own house. You can both pack your bags now and leave please.'

'You want have a fucking fight with me geezer.'

At this point I told Helen to go and call the police whilst standing my ground to not let the idiot think he was intimidating me. The main strategy, although preparing for a physical fight, was to avoid the situation deteriorating further and just get the couple out of the house as soon as possible.

'Come on mate. Let's fucking kick off. You think you're fucking hard do yer? You wanna fight me yeh? Come on then?'

'Just pack your bags and leave,' I responded as I wedged my foot in the door so that he couldn't trash the room as he collected his stuff.

'You're fucking forgetting something you are. I know where you fucking live. Do you want my London crew down to break your fucking legs do yer?'

Helen reappeared at this point to say that the police were on their way which, thankfully, led them to start getting their bags together properly. The threats and abuse, however, continued until the police appeared about five to ten minutes later. All talk of 'London hatchet crews' were then replaced, miraculously, by calm protestations of innocence. Maybe it was inevitable that the police at some point would have to be called. Hopefully, though, it will not be too regular an occurrence for the future. Otherwise the office job may be a more appealing lifestyle after all.

Saturday 11th December

6.45am this morning the doorbell is continuously rung until I go up and see what is happening.

'Remember me do yer? You'll never fucking forget me you wanker.'

Sunday 12th December

'Oh thank god we have finally found you,' a couple said laughing as they turned up a few hours late for a booking. 'It has been an absolute nightmare finding the place. We couldn't remember the name of your B&B and had forgotten to write it down. We knew it was something *fishy* in the title so we tried the "Dolphin" first. Really hoped it wasn't that place though because the windows were broken on the top floor and the owner had odd teeth sticking out to one side!'

'Well, all of our windows are intact and hopefully my teeth are straight enough for you,' I told them, flashing my best smile as I spoke.

Monday 13th December

'We were a bit naughty last night,' a couple said to me at breakfast this morning.

'Really?' I replied with a sense of anticipation.

'Went for a nice meal at that Thai restaurant you recommended and ended up ordering a second bottle of wine! We hardly ever drink that much.'

'Oh well. You are on holiday. You're entitled to push the boat out a little,' I told them, not adding that at least the third bottle would be my own personal definition of indulgence.

'I suppose that means we were binge drinking,' they giggled. 'Oops. Just lost ten thousand brain cells each.'

Not sure whether the ten thousand brain cells lost per drinking session has any scientific basis or is just a common myth but, if true, it would mean I would be losing around a million brain cells a year on the present (surely ridiculously low?) definition of binge drinking. Wow. That's twenty million brain cells already gone in the course of my drinking career. Now, do you start in the first place with a hundred million or hundred billion cells? It could be a crucial difference in what percentage of my brain has so far been wasted away.

Tuesday 14th December

Should our gay neighbours know that the sales rep for the laundry company most of us use is slightly homophobic or would that just bring up unnecessary negativity?

'There are so many gay people in Brighton aren't there? And especially in Kemp Town running the B&B's and small hotels? It's a real nice change to come to a B&B with a *normal* straight couple running it. It should be good for you though, I guess, in terms of business - the fact that you're not gay?'

'What do you mean? That all the prejudiced straight people will come and stay with us?'

'I certainly think there're a lot of people that wouldn't like to stay in a gay house.'

'Well we're not the "only straights in the village" by any means and we don't want any homophobic people staying with us regardless.'

Wednesday 15th December

Now I'm sure there are a lot of people who have had a similar frustrating experience but it is almost impossible to obtain accommodation on the weekends in Brighton unless you book for a minimum of two nights. The demand is so high that it would be ridiculous to check in one batch of people on the Friday and then change all the rooms and wait in for another batch to arrive on Saturday. Why double the workload for no reason? Frustrating as it may be, however, it is equally exasperating having to explain why every week to indignant and uppity people.

'We are going to the theatre and only want to stay for one night. What about all those people who don't want to stay for two nights? What are they supposed to do? You are a B&B aren't you? Surely then we can stay just for the night. This is absolutely outrageous.'

'As I've already explained there is a greater demand for two night stays than one and we are always oversubscribed anyway at the weekends.'

'Well it doesn't say anything about this requirement on your website.'

'It does actually state it clearly. I wrote the website myself and I check and update the details regularly.'

'I'll be contacting the local tourist authority about this. You shouldn't be allowed to get away with ripping people off like this.'

'We are a simply a private business offering a decent service and we do not force anybody to stay with us. You are welcome to set up your own B&B if you like to provide for all those wanting only one night. Last time I checked the government wasn't looking to set up state-run establishments to do the same.'

'Oh good riddance to your nasty B&B.' Phone slammed down.

Thursday 16th December

It's interesting how many people come away for a break but obviously still cling on to the familiarity of what they know and their old routines. Brighton is famous for it's independent shops and numerous cafes and restaurants, and takes pride in not representing a 'clone' experience that most other towns and cities in the UK now offer. Why then, for the second time in the last few weeks, would a guest immediately ask me on arrival where they can find the nearest Wetherspoons because 'we want to get some food and you know exactly what you're getting there.' Surely it is worth just a small look around first before going for exactly the same *burger and beer* option you have back home every other week? At least try some local fish and chips caught fresh out of the sea - well, fresh from some places anyway.

Friday 17th December

Infidelity is not any of a hoteliers' business but it doesn't mean we have to play along cheerfully with adulterers, especially those being overly smug with their indiscretion.

'I'm going to a conference in Brighton with a work colleague [separate married names] and would like to reserve a double room for three nights. [Then in hushed tone] You couldn't do us a little favour as well? Could you make the receipt out as *two single* rooms not *one double*. The company is expecting two singles but, you know, that can be our little secret hey?'

The couple when they arrived yesterday, despite being in their early forties, were like a pair of overexcited teenagers unable to disguise their glee at being away together. And the man, wearing a suit and overpowering aftershave, also tried to impress by telling me about his sports car.

'I've parked my car in the NCP for the whole three days rather than on the street. It's safer there because it's a convertible MGF,' he volunteered to me with a raised eyebrow. 'I've taken all my expensive gadgets out though.'

The *Gordon Gecko* wannabe style continued today as conference itinerary was loudly discussed in the dining room for all others to hear.

'This is really cutting edge stuff. It is going to revolutionise the industry. Let me show you who the speakers are. Real big names in America ... We're going to need a taxi for the conference centre as well.'

'It's probably quicker and easier to walk actually. It's just a few minutes walk along the seafront. And it's nice and sunny outside.'

'We'll take the taxi thanks. All on expenses and we want to arrive in style,' he said with a wink.

Saturday 18ᵗʰ December

Should the hotelier pamper the guests or is it the other way round? We let an Irish couple leave their suitcases for a few hours after check out because their flight back to Dublin was not until the evening. When they came back later they had brought a big bunch of flowers and an expensive box of chocolates for us.

'Honestly there is no need for presents. Especially such nice ones. It's quite a normal part of the job to store luggage for guests.'

'No, no. You must accept the gifts. We insist. It was a really lovely gesture to look after our bags and the stay has been fantastic. Thank you very much.'

Oh well. You can only argue so much. No choice but to say yes.

Sunday 19th December

'Homosexuality is only a disease of the West. It doesn't exist in any Muslim countries.' Ha! I knew this couldn't possibly be true and now I have proof.

'This is a very special few days away for me and my partner. Please could you make sure it is a double bed *not* a twin,' a Saudi Arabian man, working and living in London, had insisted upon repeatedly when booking a room.

When the 'partners' arrived yesterday it was two men, both Saudis, who were clearly a gay couple (although my Muslim friend from the past would no doubt still insist they were only 'friends.') More interesting, however, than the very existence of gay Muslims, was the extreme concern shown at breakfast this morning about pork being in the vegetarian breakfast.

'We want to order two vegetarian breakfasts but are you *absolutely* sure there is no pork in the vegetarian sausage?'

'Of course not. Vegetarian means no meat whatsoever.'

'So there is *definitely* no pork in the sausage?'

'100% not. You can trust me, honest. Vegetarian by definition means that it is meat free.'

'And that includes *no* pork?'

'Yes. Definitely no pork. I can show you the packet. They are made from soya products.'

'So there is no pork in these, *only* soya?' he asked again whilst closely inspecting the packet of our vegetarian sausages.

'Yes.'

'Yes, *only* soya and *no* pork?'

'Yes.'

'Ok. If there is *no* pork then we will have two vegetarian breakfasts please.'

The plates, about thirty seconds after the 'vegetarian' breakfasts had been served, were carried back down the corridor and into the kitchen.

'Are you sure this is the vegetarian sausage because it looks exactly like one with pork in it?'

'Yes. That's a vegetarian sausage. They deliberately make these vegetarian products to look similar to meat versions.'

'But there is no pork in them?'

'No.'

After breakfast, clearing up all the dishes, we noticed that both their plates had the vegetarian sausages left completely untouched. Obviously not reassured enough that there was no pork in them! It just shows though how strongly people can feel about strictly following certain tenets of their culture/religion. In this case, of course, gay sex is evidently not deemed as sinful as eating pork.

Monday 20th December

Surely the simple technological invention of the toast rack has reached advanced capitalism in North America?

A young Canadian couple are absolutely fascinated by our toast racks which, according to them, do not exist in Canada. Our toast racks are a fairly plain stainless steel design, certainly not anything fancy, but for three mornings in a row this couple has not stopped mentioning them.

'Gee. We have never seen anything like this before in our lives. It must be an English thing to store toast in this way. They are so cute though and it's such a good idea. Could we have one or buy one from you to take back and show our mom?'

Tuesday 21st December

Brighton, along with other populations along the south coast, has a 'Burning the Clocks' procession and ceremony to mark the winter solstice and the end of days getting shorter. Officially the event is also described as an 'antidote to the excesses of commercial Christmas' and has an atmospheric pagan ritual feel with garish lantern effigies paraded through the streets accompanied by drumming and pipes. Tens of thousands turn out and the procession ends on the beach where all the lanterns are piled up and set alight in front of a giant sun symbol before fireworks explode.

Wednesday 22nd December

Now I wonder if our American guest at the moment is a Republican or a Democrat? Hank, from Arizona, always wears a cowboy hat and shoes and the 'Western' style shirts with tassels hanging down. In his late fifties, with masses of bushy nasal and ear hair which are very hard to ignore, Hank reminds me somewhat of 'Boss Hogg' from *The Dukes of Hazard*. Talking incessantly, and notwithstanding the nasal/ear hair distraction, it seems impossible to ever steer the 'conversation' with Hank away from the same theme of how 'us' Anglos are getting overrun by Latinos and Asians.

'Whites are becoming a minority in the US now and the same thing is going to happen here by the looks of things to me. In Arizona and California we got millions of Latinos pouring in every year.'

'I quite like Mexican food though so that's at least one plus,' I tried to deflect him with earlier. 'And what's your plans for today - off sightseeing anywhere?'

Hank, completely ignoring my question, literally exploded into an even greater rage at this point that I wasn't quite expecting. His face turned beetroot red, hands gesticulated wildly and spit came flying out of his mouth with every word.

'And those **Ay-rabs**. They know now if they try and mess with us we'll break their darn necks,' he shouted as his hands mimicked a chicken getting its neck snapped violently.

'We aint taking any shit from **Ay-rabs**. We'll bomb em' all. They gotta know they can't mess with us and get away with it.'

Thursday 23rd December

No doubt to the disapproval of Hank, who thankfully has now checked-out anyway, a man from Bahrain arrived today with his Scottish girlfriend who is out working in the Middle East (though very well-to-do types I'm sure Hank would still disapprove of such mixed race relationships.) However, strangely echoing similar themes to Hank, the man from Bahrain started talking himself about immigration and how it is having a negative effect on Britain, which he compared unfavourably to Bahrain.

'We don't have the same problems that you have because we make sure that no sub-standard immigrants - Asians and Blacks - can get into our country permanently. You let anyone in here and it's causing problems.'

Great. Yesterday I get an American cowboy complaining about Latinos and Asians and threatening to break 'Ay-rabs' necks. Now I have an Arab man complaining about 'substandard Asian and Black people' in Britain. What next?

Continuing to espouse the virtues of Bahrain, although conveniently not mentioning the added bonus of oil revenue billions, he also gave me a philosophical analogy to explain the secret of the Gulf States' success.

'Life is like a piano - how you play it is what tune you get out.'

'That's ok,' I responded, 'so long as you own a piano in the first place.'

Friday 24ᵗʰ December

We sent an email to say 'sorry but we are fully booked' for dates wanted next week.

'You fucking wankers,' was the reply that came back.

Very nice. Seasons greetings to you as well. I'll look forward even more now to being completely closed for Christmas.

Friday 31st December

Yes, some nice time off, and especially so after six consecutive weeks of working (seven days a week). And, yes, the belly has also expanded a few inches due to an excessive drip feed of constant eating and drinking. Still that's what Christmas is for isn't it? Reopen now however for New Years Eve because it's one of the busiest times of the year. Yippee!

JANUARY

BBC types and leather bondage?

Saturday 1st January

I was talking to Helen yesterday in our lounge/reception room about a rather surreal dream I'd had the previous night about stabbing small freshwater crocodiles to death. Following the rather brutal description of my annihilation of these creatures (which rarely ever attack humans incidentally), I made a joke about the dream perhaps being a metaphor for my subconscious feelings towards the guests. Unfortunately, however, as soon as the sentence was finished I realised a couple were standing by the doorway waiting to ask a question. As they pretended to have not overheard the dubious self-analysis of the state of my psyche I casually answered their question with perhaps an overly warm smile. Maybe my dream interpretation did have a bigger impact than I realised though because the couple never came down to breakfast this morning, and deliberately checked out without seeing us!

Sunday 2nd January

Some of the inequities of the global economy were brought sharply home today when a doctor from Uganda arrived for an international medical conference.

'My deposit only covers the first night stay of the accommodation not the second night also? I have to pay double the amount to stay for both nights? Oh no, please tell me this is a mistake. No way. No way. Surely it can't be that much for a hotel room?'

'Well the price actually includes a very large discount already for single occupancy of a double room. We would barely break even at that price for two nights. A dorm bed with no breakfast in a backpackers would cost more.'

In direct exchange rate terms the average income here is about fifty times higher than in Uganda. I imagine if I booked abroad the equivalent of a £40 a night hotel room here and it was already costing me £2,000, it would be fairly painful to then find out the actual cost had moved up to £4,000 a night.

Monday 3rd January

Who said we now live in a classless society? Two middle aged women guests from Luton, perhaps not the most well spoken or best dressed, prove social division is still alive and kicking. However, even if people do still judge books by their gold jewellery and tracksuit covers, surely unsolicited abuse isn't called for?

'Had a great time in the pub opposite last night. Really good atmosphere. Made to feel very welcome. A lot nicer here than back where we're from. You wouldn't believe what happened to us last week. We were in a pub in the centre of Luton, quietly minding our own business, when a group of drunk students started shouting abuse. Such things as "Shouldn't you two be back at home watching Coronation Street." They thought it was hilarious, rolling around laughing at us.'

Surely it's a bit of an oxymoron for students at Luton University to regard themselves as so elitist? Anyhow, certainly not an isolated incident. I recall a letter being sent to the student newspaper in Sheffield only a few years back, which complained about the expansion of higher education and the "middle class now having to mix with too many mining village idiots."

Tuesday 4th January

When guests are alone in the dining room the stories often start flowing. Two English couples sitting together having breakfast today and one of the men relayed a story about an Irish friend who had a Swedish girlfriend who 'spoke good English but not quite good enough.'

'On the farm where my friend lived it was common parlance for all the guys working to refer often to the horses as "stupid c**ts." His Swedish girlfriend, however, did not really grasp the meaning of the phrase. After staying a few weeks, sitting round the dinner table one night with my mate's family, she casually referred to his dad in conversation as a stupid c**t.'

'Oh goodness me,' the Irish mum exclaimed in horror. 'You mustn't use such language.'

'What do you mean? What's wrong with saying *stupid 'c*nt'*.

'Don't say that word, please. Do you not know what it means?'

'Yes. It means that you are a "naughty horse."'

'Oh goodness me child, no it does not mean that.'

'What then?'

'You're *sitting* on it,' the Irish mum said flustered whilst pointing downwards.

'I'm sorry I still don't understand,' the Swedish girl responded as she looked confusingly down towards her chair.

'It's in your knickers,' was the final exasperated rasp from the Irish mum.

Wednesday 5th January

In contrast to the room of the average British guest, which frequently is left in varying degrees of mess, our German cousins appear (from our limited anecdotal evidence anyhow) to fit their much caricatured stereotype for 'orderliness.' Not only though are German rooms left neat and tidy, but the beds always seem to be made identically also with the duvet folded over in half and then rotated ninety degrees. What could be the origins and social significance of this disciplined bed-making procedure? Perhaps it has been vigorously taught and learnt for generations in the German Scouts/Guides rulebook or in national service? Either way maybe it's something we need to consider adding to our own national curriculum to make sure Britain doesn't fall behind in international competitiveness?

Incidentally, on the subject of efficiency, German men always sit down apparently when using the toilet even when it's just for a wee. Obviously this creates a more orderly environment where no urine is ever splashed accidentally and no arguments exist about 'the toilet seat being left up.' As such chivalrous male behaviour is obviously very conducive for both hygiene and the creation of harmony between the sexes, perhaps this is another area of German culture that seriously needs to be considered for adoption over here?

Thursday 6th January

A few small words of wisdom, especially from those with greater life experience, can help jolt the senses. An English woman guest in her late fifties, who has lived in Australia for the past thirty years, has come back to England for a few weeks to meet her daughter for the first ever time who was adopted at birth. The woman has emphysema and implies that this is probably going to be her final visit back, and only time of meeting her daughter, before returning to Australia. At breakfast she sat at the table closest to the kitchen and overheard Helen and me a bit stressed over nothing much important and snapping at each other. When leaving she thanked us for breakfast and gently offered the advice, 'remember that life is very short, you should try and enjoy it as much as possible.'

Friday 7th January

B&B/hotel guests and electric macerator toilets are not a good combination!

'Please do not flush any non-tissue objects - sanitary products, condoms, cotton wool etc - otherwise the toilet will block. Thank you for your cooperation.'

Of course this notice is often ignored. Today, however, things went one better than normal. A guest, after flushing a sanitary towel, somehow managed to then keep the connected sink tap running without realising the blockage. Surely when a full toilet load of crap starts seeping over the top of the toilet bowl you soon notice - especially when the sewage water spills all the way out and also soaks the room carpet?

'Sorry, I just had the tap running whilst brushing my teeth. I didn't realise there was a problem until my feet started getting wet.'

Needless to say that five minutes before breakfast was furthermore not the best time to hear about such a problem.

Saturday 8th January

'Well my daughter smokes so not sure whether to book. I know she would prefer a smoking room. Oh what to do, what to do? Ok, I'll book the room anyway. It should be alright.'

My apprehension about this booking was not quelled in any way when the mum and daughter turned up today for their twin room.

'Cor this is well nice. We normally stay in right old dumps,' were the daughter's first words on seeing the room.

A couple of hours later, whilst showing other guests upstairs, I immediately smelt cigarette smoke in the corridor emanating from the mum and daughter's room.

'Sorry but even smoking out the window is not allowed.'

'Ok. Alright. Sorry.'

About three hours later someone started banging loudly on the reception/lounge. When I opened the door the mum was angrily staring at me with a packed suit-case in the corridor. She then slammed her room key into my hand and launched into an apoplectic tirade.

'What you been spying on me and my daughter have you? What you been out in the street looking up at us, yeh? You telling me you can smell smoke from all the way down here? You got no right to be snooping outside our room.'

'Please calm down. I smelt smoke outside your room earlier when I was showing people into the room next door to yours. It's not a big deal we just don't want anyone smoking in the house. That's it.'

'Well that's **not** it as far as we're concerned. You can **stick** your room. We don't want it. We're not being spied upon whilst we're on holiday trying to enjoy ourselves. What kind of place is this? Snooping. Looking up at us from the street. Hanging outside our room. It's not on.'

And with that she picked up her suitcase and stormed out the front door with her daughter who was already waiting outside. Although completely astonished and slightly shell-shocked by her tirade, at least they had both gone – and the room had been paid in full as well so good riddance really.

Sunday 9th January

Is it the guests or the hosts who should provide a welcome bottle of wine?

'We have brought this bottle of Rioja as a present for you. It is from our home region in northern Spain,' announced a couple when they first arrived to check-in.

'Oh that's very kind of you. We don't normally expect guests to bring gifts. Thank you.'

There were a few brief seconds of careful reflection when the wine was nearly refused. But, of course, not wanting to appear rude there was no choice but to humbly accept their offering. In fact the entire bottle has just been finished off this evening and quite a nice 'drop' it was too.

Monday 10th January

Now I'm really starting to appreciate guests from the Mediterranean? Today it was the turn of the Maltese to arrive bearing (unsolicited, honestly!) a wrapped-up present before even setting foot in the door. The gift, when opened, turned out to be a sturdy leather-bound diary decorated with Maltese imprints. Perhaps it is a more normal custom in the Mediterranean to give presents to strangers? Either way it certainly works as a pleasant ice-breaker. Maybe I should just drop any 'uptight' embarrassment and expect it as normal that all guests bring presents on arrival? A new cultural import, like the recent phenomenon of kissing strangers on the cheek. We provide you with bed and breakfast and you must bring a hand-picked gift (preferably wrapped) in addition to the standard money payment. Those are the new rules.

Tuesday 11th January

In keeping with a city that regularly records the highest 'green' vote in elections, a number of B&Bs/hotels in Brighton specifically market themselves as very environmentally wholesome. A couple arrived for us today, however, who had decided to check-out early from their nearby 'Green' establishment.

'The room was bloody freezing. We knew it was an environmentally-friendly place but still expected to have some heating on when the weather is this cold.'

Coincidentally I had just read a 'Green your House' article which stated that the average indoor temperature of a UK house has increased from thirteen degrees Celsius in the 1970s to nineteen degrees now. As the resulting higher energy use was cited as a significant contributor to greenhouse gas emissions, the article also advocated that everyone should turn down their thermostats a few notches. Surely a bit of a tricky 'green' dilemma though for B&Bs/hotels which still seek to be *modern and stylish*? Not the catchiest marketing strategy - 'A semi-cold, but eco-friendly place to stay.'

Wednesday 12th January

A letter arrived today with our house number and street name but wrongly addressed as 'avenue.' The letter read:

'Dear Hilary,

I hope you are all keeping well and had a lovely Christmas.

Again I let you all down and am so sorry.

For no reasons I went off the rails and the demons took over.

I'm now back in recovery - to continue this struggle once again. From the 17th January I will be in a retreat.

The address is St Benedicts, 1 Manor R.D., Brighton.

You can phone or visit if you would like to.

Mum'

Sorry but we were unable to find the correct address to forward the letter. So if you are Hilary and reading this, your mum did try to make contact with you.

Thursday 13th January

'Hello, anybody in?' Helen said audibly today, whilst cleaning, as she gave the usual courtesy knock ahead of entering a guest bedroom. Helen didn't know, however, that I was already inside the room doing the service.

'Sorry, but could you come back later,' I replied in a shrill and loud put on guest voice. 'We're just having a lovely bit of nookie at the moment so it's a bit inconvenient. Thank you.'

As I then opened the door to greet Helen, beaming widely at my own joke, the grin turned quickly to embarrassment as I immediately saw two other guests just passing by at the exact same moment.

Friday 14th January

The lifestyle of the British *yoof,* judging anyhow by the comments of a middle aged male American guest, are somewhat different from back in the States.

'Scott. Those streets out there are getting weird again. I'm closing this door and no way risking going back out. What's going on? There are twelve year olds roaming all over the place getting absolutely drunk out of their minds. It's scary.'

'Well it's nice to know you are getting familiar with our culture. We like to get the kids started young so they can carry on our traditions. People worry otherwise that the binge-drinking custom may die out in the future.'

Saturday 15th January

It is useful, when a booking is made, to jot down any background information gained about a guest to help with conversation. Today, the reservations diary stated that our one arrival was 'going to Brighton Dome to see a concert.'

'Ah, that's good,' I thought to myself. 'The London Philharmonic Orchestra has been playing there all week. These guests are unlikely to be too rowdy or troublesome.'

A short while later, already on the computer, I decided to have a quick look at the Brighton Dome's website. The Orchestra had actually finished playing the night before and instead there was a gig on tonight by punk rock band 'Rancid,' whose track titles include *Time Bomb*; *Nihilism*; *Junkie Man*; and *Rejected*. Now, especially remembering my own grungy past in the early nineties, it would have been unjust to be too apprehensive in advance of our 'rancid' arrivals. And, in all fairness, when the couple showed up (replete with Mohicans and full punk regalia), both were very nice and friendly. What type of guest, though, would be more likely to throw the clichéd 'television out of the hotel window' - punk rockers or classical music fans?

Sunday 16th January

Our punk rocker guests, of course, left the room in a perfectly fine condition and 'really enjoyed' the gig and staying with us. There you go - 'never judge a rancid book by its cover.'

Monday 17th January

Is 'throwing the TV out of the hotel window' just an urban myth or does it actually happen? And, if it does, apart from the wanton criminal damage aspect, surely it could be a bit dangerous if the TV lands on someone's head? To fret about such trivial concerns in the first place, though, probably means you are not really the type to best understand such wild abandon.

Tuesday 18th January

Another anecdote to bolster stereotype prejudice.

'It will just be me today,' an Australian man, with a broad Ozzie accent, announced loudly as he walked into the dining room which was half full with other guests already eating.

'The wife won't be coming down because she's not feeling too good. Got a bit of diarrhoea,' he further divulged, offering a bit more information than everyone else wanted to hear.

Later on in the evening both the man and his wife were in the hallway whilst some other guests were also passing.

'Hiya,' the Australian woman said to me. 'I'm feeling a bit better now. Jeez, though, I was really rough earlier. Should make it to Brekkie tomorrow hopefully. Just hope that everything won't be chucked back up if I eat.'

Wednesday 19th January

Running a B&B is rapidly forcing me to start getting better at DIY, even though I have spent my whole life hating maintenance and anything practical - perhaps the wrong job has been picked after all?

It was raining quite hard today when I showed two young women into a twin room on the top floor only to be greeted by water pouring through the ceiling above the window. Great.

'Oh, I think we may have a problem here.'

Luckily we were able to switch the guests to another room which wasn't semi-flooded. And although there was some satisfaction from clearing the blocked gutter causing the problem, it's not really my idea of fun to hang over a roof - five storeys up in heavy rain - getting caked in mud.

Thursday 20th January

Last night we were invited to the launch party of the newly refurbished hotel next door which is re-opening as an exclusive boutique establishment with a number of rooms having a 'Gay Bondage' theme.

'Their guests will have lots of money to pay such high prices. You needn't worry in case you're apprehensive. It won't cause any trouble. Apparently they are hoping to attract lots of "BBC types" down from London,' our other gay neighbours had told us.

When the new 'Bondage Hotel' website was launched a few weeks ago, however, the 'reassuring' opinions of our neighbours appeared to have changed slightly.

'Honestly. You wouldn't expect such things really in the street you live in. It makes you want to move to Devon,' was the new response.

On the home page of the 'Bondage Hotel' website is a semi-naked picture of our new neighbour dressed in a leather gimp mask with breathing apparatus. Along with the 'dungeon' room, and 'skinhead' room, there is also a themed 'yellow' room - yes, try and use your bondage imagination and you will be correct. In all of the rooms you are further able to hire slings to hang from the ceilings (not sure about the exact sinister nature of this supposedly popular bondage device but that is probably just my naivety.)

When we arrived at the launch party there were lots of middle aged men, many of them wearing leather chaps with only g-strings at the back, and Helen was literally the only woman there. The bar host, bare-chested and replete with studded dog-collar, bull nose ring, knee high boots and leather hot pants was very generous though in keeping our glasses topped up with champagne and wine and it was not long before we started mingling socially. Our 'non-bondage' gay neighbours did not seem too impressed with some of the outfits judging by their comments.

'Fancy exposing your backside like that when you have cellulite.'

In the toilet there was a full length naked photographic imprint (apart from the leather chaps of course) of our other new neighbour from behind. Although not accustomed to staring at images of nude men, especially whilst holding myself, after my fifth glass of champagne and third toilet visit it did start to feel more normal - please, I just have a weak bladder not latent homosexuality!

The hotel was full with paying guests on its opening night but this did not prevent our new neighbour (the one imprinted on the website, not the toilet wall) giving us a full tour round. In the 'dungeon' room were two shy, timid guys dressed in rubber all-in-ones. Both looked more like middle aged accountants than the now notorious 'BBC types.' We were quite disappointed really. The sinister mental image of some bleak, sadistic chamber was in reality just a double bunk-bed with a space underneath and some flimsy looking bars. How disappointing! This sadomasochist lark is obviously not all it's cracked up to be.

Could there possibly be some sort of scientific correlation, given that nearly all the men at the party were middle class and professional, between a fetish for gay bondage and social background? In the same sort of way, perhaps, that 90% of anorexic girls are from a middle class background? Maybe there is some link between high-achieving parents who have similar expectations and aspirations for their children, and a variety of behaviours caused from the stress of such pressures? Alternatively, of course, some people may simply get their kicks from pretending to be locked underneath a bunk bed whilst wearing rubber?

Friday 21st January

Most writers probably read their work out loud when editing to make sure it sounds correct. How many writers, however, repetitively chant slightly different permutations of 'gay bondage theme' sentences not realising a rather conservative looking straight couple are waiting nearby to see them?

'Semi-naked picture of our new neighbour dressed in a leather gimp mask with breathing apparatus …Bondage room, Yellow room … Use your bondage imagination … BBC types …'

In such circumstances it is surely best to not try and offer an explanation? More fun to leave people to ponder with confusion on the situation. Just expecting though an imminent review now on *tripadvisor* that says 'nice rooms but a rather odd owner who can be overheard talking about gay bondage to himself.'

Saturday 22nd January

A cargo ship sunk off the coast of Dorset a couple of days ago, which has resulted in two thousand tonnes of treated timber being strewn along the whole southern coastline. Brighton has not been spared, and there are masses of timber piled up on the beach, with JCB's brought in to try and clean up. As well as (illegal) bonfires being set up, others have used the timber planks to spell out large messages such as; 'Imagine if this was oil.'

Although also much talk in Brighton recently about re-building the collapsed *West Pier*, there appears to be no connection with all the wood that has been delivered

– well, no allen keys, fittings, or instruction leaflet have been supplied with the wood anyhow.

Sunday 23rd January

The police and an ambulance had to be called out last night because some idiot had tried to lever themselves up onto the first floor balcony of one of our neighbours. However, instead of managing to break into our neighbours house as planned, all they succeeded in doing was slipping down onto the railings below and causing themselves a serious injury. Should this elicit any sympathy or is it merely a case of poetic justice?

Monday 24th January

We have an American man staying with us who works as a 'high school' teacher in California, a job that he describes as "absolute insanity." However, similar to the other American guest a few weeks earlier, it seems that our binge-drinking yoofs and city centre streets are the biggest 'insanity' of all.

"At least our teenagers don't have access to alcohol. I'll be back before night to avoid them. That was pretty scary out there last night.'

Tuesday 25th January

'We are looking for a room and also we have a very small Chihuahua. We know it says on your website that you do not accept pets but the dog is only small and would be no problem at all. Would you be ok with that?'

Chihuahua's may well be the smallest breed of dog in the world but they are still an animal! If the woman could 100% guarantee the dog was potty trained, would not shed any hairs, make any noise, scratch up the carpet or leave any smells ... then still the dog would not be allowed to stay. 'Sorry, but we do not accept pets.'

Wednesday 26th January

A rather nervous young Czech woman staying by herself, not particularly fluent in English, walked awkwardly into the dining room. Although we have a choice of eggs, bacon, sausages, vegetarian sausages, tomatoes, hash browns, baked beans, croissants, a selection of cereals, fresh fruit, yoghurts, and toast with jams/marmalades, she screws up her face with a look of utter disgust at our menu.

'Agh. I do not like any of this food. Could you just make me some potatoes and cheese?'

Thursday 27th January

There are twenty-six characters in the Latin alphabet compared to over forty-seven thousand Han characters in the Chinese alphabet. Of course, though, having a lot less characters to master still doesn't make learning a completely alien language any easier.

'Please can I speak to Scottandhelen.'

'Yes, this is Scott.'

'No, I have had an email and I need to speak to a Scot-tandhelen, please.'

'Yes my name is Scott. And my partner's name is Helen. So I can help you.'

'Oh, I see. I'm sorry I thought Scottandhelen was one person.'

Well actually when you work with your partner twenty-four hours a day, seven days week, it can often feel like you are becoming the same person! In fact there is no 'us' anymore, only one person henceforth to be named as 'Scottandhelen.'

Friday 28th January

Nottingham Forest are playing Brighton tomorrow and two couples arrived today with the men here 'to watch the football' while the women are planning to 'go off and do some shopping.'

'What team do you support then?' asked one of the men as I showed them upstairs.

After many years in a variety of different social situations I am now used to the fact that asking 'which football team you follow' is the primary ice breaker conversation starter - or perhaps the only conversation entirely - for a large percentage of the male population.

'Ah, I'm a Liverpool man myself,' I replied, lying.

Luckily the prevarication did the trick and we then had a couple of minutes of friendly knockabout 'football' banter. Being a former player I was able to keep the chat going along adequately and also to refute any charge of being some 'non-sporty *wus*.' The problem, however, is that I have never supported any team. Shock.

Horror. Some men just can't comprehend it. And, I have now learnt, it is always better to respond to the *ice breaker conversation* with a made-up team (it can vary depending on your mood), thus ensuring social ostracising does not occur. What kind of normal straight bloke, after all, who is not some sort of namby-pamby weirdo, does not support a football team?

Saturday 29th January

'And are you in town for anything special or is it just a short break away?'

'We're here to attend a funeral actually.'

'Oh, I'm sorry to hear that,' I said before the conversation then went a bit uncomfortably quiet. Not sure whether the man was interested in football or not otherwise I would have asked him what team he supported.

Sunday 30th January

Despite the potential statistical weight of evidence we are not animal abuse offenders! For the third time now in the last eight weeks we have had to call the RSPCA out to rescue a bird stuck injured in our backyard. And, honestly, we are not weirdos that get sadistic kicks from knocking birds out of the sky and then pretending to be interested in their saviour.

The previous two occasions, apart from the seagull that nearly landed on my head like an Exocet missile out of nowhere, have been fairly straightforward. Cover the birds for protection (with a plastic laundry basket in our case) and provide a saucer of water. A RSPCA officer, able to avoid being bitten when handling, then comes to take the bird for rehabilitation or to be put down mercifully. Not sure whether a murderous Darwinian cull or just compassionate euthanasia but apparently, if left exposed, birds (especially pigeons) will seek to kill an injured member of their fellow species. We were able to witness such an attempted killing, in dramatic fashion, whilst trying to serve breakfast this morning.

Discovering an injured pigeon outside your kitchen door just as you start preparing breakfast is not ideal - particularly when the pigeon tries to scurry in whenever the door is opened. Equally problematic is a pigeon preventing itself being covered with a laundry basket by wedging itself behind the door when chased out. Greater chaos ensues though when a gang of other pigeons undertake numerous waves of noisy murderous attacks when the dining room is full of guests. I've never done the training course for surreptitiously shooing away a bloodthirsty gang of birds every few minutes whilst simultaneously trying to prevent another bird running into the kitchen.

Monday 31st January

Why does every older generation think that life was so much better in the 'good old days' not realising that those days were mainly good only because they coincided with their own youthful vigour, excitement and optimism – and nothing, of course, to do with present failing health and disillusioned, unfulfilled lifetime dreams.

'I don't know what the world is coming to these days,' an elderly guest said today, in true cliché form, during a conversation which was always destined to become *an old git* moan. 'It never used to be this bad when we were growing up.'

Given that every older generation since the beginning of time has thought the same thing regardless it's amazing really how human evolution has not regressed back into some sea bacteria life form?

FEBRUARY

Allo, I am French

Tuesday 1st February

Poor personal hygiene is not the most endearing personality trait. An Austrian family are staying - mum, dad
and teenage daughter - all of whom are very nice people
with friendly smiles and a warm demeanour. The only
problem, however, is that all three of them happen to
share an unfortunate family characteristic of absolutely
reeking of an unpleasant smell that is a cross somewhere
between bad body odour and urine. No matter how
congenial the personalities, it is extremely hard to feel
really amicable towards people when your overriding
thoughts during a conversation are 'bloody hell I can't
believe how much you lot stink.'

It's also a bit of a concern though because after the
Austrian family has walked up or down the stairs, the
whole B&B seems to be contaminated for a good fifteen
or twenty minutes with their lingering smelliness. Helen
now is constantly checking the stairs and hallway, just in
case they have recently entered or gone out, to then
quickly spray some air freshener to try to nullify the
pong. This paranoia was furthermore enhanced this
morning when we were showing in some new arrivals
just seconds after 'the Austrians' had left. We wanted, of
course, to explain to our new guests that the awful
stench was not our fault. It was decided however that
drawing extra attention to the unpleasant smell of our
B&B would probably not be the ideal welcome.

'Apologies for the terrible smell, it's not our hygiene
standards, honest. There are just some extremely smelly

guests in the room next door to you that stink of urine.'
Not really what guests want to hear on arrival is it?

Inside 'the Austrians' gut wrenching room - leaving
aside the additional embarrassment of them walking
into the dining room as everyone else *was* enjoying
breakfast - we found three separate items of underwear
(one each for mum, dad and daughter) hanging over the
towel rails drying. Perhaps that was the source of the
smell - one change of underwear that only gets hand
washed once a week when on holiday?

Wednesday 2nd February

Our gay vegetarian neighbours invited us around for
dinner this evening.

'Yes, vegetarian food is fine. We're not complete
carnivorous addicts. In fact we often go to *Food for
Friends* [a well known vegetarian restaurant in 'The
Lanes.'] It's one of our favourites.'

'Well we agree that the food is excellent but the
restaurant is far too *lesbian* for our tastes. You know –
a wholesome, holier than thou, feminine – type of a
place.'

Wow. It was just a restaurant that had good food and
service as far as we knew. A restaurant can be too feminine or even too *lesbian*? We obviously need to tune our
gaydar in more – start assessing eateries on the basis of a
gender/sexuality dimension.

'Women really *aren't* our favourite guests to be
honest,' our neighbours earnestly told us later. 'So many
times we have had to wash towels on sixty/ninety
degrees to get make-up stains out. It's so annoying.'

I wonder how important your sexual orientation could be in influencing your attitude towards guests? Personally I much prefer to have female guests stay. Which gender is cleaner, better behaved, politer, friendlier, and which is smellier, macho, and frequently more alcohol-soaked?

Perhaps there is some underlying Freudian dynamic at work that makes me canonize the 'feminine' whilst subconsciously wanting to get males 'off my turf?' This seems to particularly apply also to smell. The 'scent of a woman' guest usually makes me feel very congenial, whereas the exact opposite occurs to any obvious masculine smell. Maybe it is these same pheromones that give my gay neighbours a completely contrary view?

Of course, when you have guests like 'the Austrians' stay, such pheromone theories go utterly out the window regardless of which sex they apply to. And, incidentally, when I mentioned the theory to Helen, she replied that she too "absolutely" preferred both the female smell and behaviour. What could that mean?

Thursday 3rd February

Is it appropriate or acceptable, when a man shares a twin room with his twelve year old daughter, to have multiple copies of The Sport newspaper left open with the usual full naked display of women? Not against the law to buy such newspapers, and probably no more than the normal 'reading' routine for the day, but should that really be something you do in front of your daughter? Perhaps, though, it is not much different from the millions of people who read our more 'upmarket' tabloids with just the *one* naked female page? It's an interesting irony too that the same tabloid newspapers that so often run vitriolic 'anti-paedophile' campaigns then glorify so much in the nakedness of a 'young sixteen year old beauty' on the next page.

Friday 4th February

Surely it's not the norm to have conversations at breakfast about male genitalia and their relative international sizes? A couple of friendly young Japanese men, exchange students keen to practise their English skills with native speakers, have been staying after spending four months at a nearby language school.

'Thank you very much Scott. We like speaking with you every morning. It's much better to speak to proper English person. In language school we not talk to English people very much, only other students.'

'That's ok. Talk away. You know the best way to learn though is to get an English girlfriend. Then you could practice a lot more,' I suggested light-heartedly.

'Get English girlfriend (much laughter). Ah. We wish we could but English girls no like us. They all think that we have very small penises,' one of them replied whilst wriggling his little finger at me.

Now not having seen a representative sample of Japanese penises to know how they measure up, nor canvassed the views of any English females, I couldn't really provide any objective counter-balancing argument. Still, I did reassure the two of them anyhow that they were wrong and literally millions of English women were waiting to be seduced by their charms.

Saturday 5th February

The American guy who is scared and horrified from his encounters with British teenagers on our streets walks in as a noisy scooter goes tearing past the B&B.

'Gee, Scott. It's amazing. They can put a man on the moon but they can't make a quiet scooter.'

Sunday 6th February

Human beings, judging from the observations made in our dining room, are most definitely territorial creatures of habit. There is about a 98% chance, once people have chosen or found a seat for themselves, that they will sit in the exact same positions on the same table the next day. Even the cramped corner table, with restricted headroom underneath a concealed fuse box, is virtually always returned to. Furthermore, if people find someone else *already* sitting on 'their' table you can often see and feel their anguished look of dispossession. If simply having breakfast from a new spatial perspective can cause so much animosity it's no wonder that so many wars have been fought in history over territory.

Anyway, in a sort of surreal reversal of this observed human psychological trait, a couple came down this morning and chose to sit at the nice window table near to the fresh flowers.

'That's where we normally like to sit,' I said, politely making conversation.

'Oh. We're ever so sorry,' was the apologetic reply as they got up to move.

'No, please. It's ok. We don't sit here whilst cooking and serving breakfast. I was merely complimenting you on your good choice of table.'

Perhaps it would have been more enjoyable to feign indignation at their outrageous audacity in sitting in our favourite place?

Monday 7th February

'My friend and I are both seventeen and want to come to Brighton to just do a bit of shopping and then stay overnight. Could you tell me please whether we are old enough to stay in your B&B?' a well spoken and polite sounding girl had asked on the phone a few days ago.

Being new to the business and not having formulated any age policy as of yet, I couldn't really see any problem with them staying, especially when she sounded very mature and sensible. Today, however, I got a call from the girl's mum asking me to cancel the booking and refund the deposit, and quite indignant that the booking had been accepted in the first place.

"She thinks she is mature, but she is not. And I really think also it's quite appalling that you were prepared to allow someone so young to stay at your establishment," I was assertively told with a distressed voice of moral outrage (or was is it condescension?)

Now this took me aback slightly. Had my actions really been so 'appalling?' Had I committed a crime? Was I some dodgy B&B owner prepared to put making money over ethics?

Surely if you are old enough to leave school, have a full time job, drive a car, and have your own children, you should be able to stay a night in a hotel by yourself after a bit of shopping?

This said, though, I was not prepared to argue against the mother's wishes and agreed to cancel and refund the booking. Probably for the best anyway with hindsight, especially after talking to our more experienced neighbours. Do we really want teenagers to stay unaccompanied in our house even if they do sound mature?

Tuesday 8th February

We had the 'vacancy' sign turned in the window today and two guys around twenty years old knocked on the door. Both were wearing tracksuits, had lots of chunky gold jewellery and a baseball cap on each. They were also both eating burgers and didn't speak at first because their mouths were too full munching away.

'Can I help you?' I asked but one of them casually raised his hand as if to say 'give us a moment' whilst they carried on eating.

Eventually, after a few big chews and a gulp down of the greasy burger, one of them bluntly said, 'Got any rooms?'

'No,' I responded.

Wednesday 9th February

How many men actually let women get away with things simply because of feminine manipulation?

'I've parked in the private car park of the offices across the road. I'll just leave the car there for the weekend - can't be bothered to mess around looking for a space on the streets,' a young attractive female guest said on arrival yesterday.

'You will probably get clamped if you leave the car there.'

'Oh I'm sure if that happens I'll be able to talk my way out of it,' she dismissed, whilst deliberately running her fingers through her hair and fluttering her eyelashes in exaggerated fashion.

This morning the same woman padded into the dining room ten minutes late for breakfast.

'Good morning. I couldn't ask a really big favour from you,' she softly asserted in the same orchestrated manner as her - *I can get whatever I want voice* - the previous day.

'My friend is feeling ever so unwell and we wondered whether it would be possible to have breakfast in the room instead of down here?'

Reluctantly, not really wanting her to think the cartoon feminine charms were influencing me, I did allow her to take some croissants up to the room - although, at least, the request for bacon sandwiches and a pot of coffee (already available to make for yourself in the room) was refused.

When we later serviced their room we found a large bottle of Bacardi that was half empty. Now would that 'feeling unwell' this morning be connected to the Bacardi or not?

Thursday 10th February

An atmospheric bar/café venue just round the corner had a *night of music, comedy and poetry* yesterday evening.

One of the poets, in between a recital, used the quote whilst elucidating on the nature of his art, 'There's no money in poetry. But then again there is no poetry in money.'

Is it poetic to metamorphose into some kind of *load-samoney* spendthrift maniac character even though your overall income hardly covers the bills and mortgage? The psychology of money seems to dictate that you feel wealthy regardless if your wallet happens to be full of cash. In fact, a fools gold mentality in the last few weeks has seen me insisting on not only buying the wine, but also paying for the bottle at least one up the list from the house red.

I have met many a Marxist academic who undoubtedly has taken some sort of perverted *poetic* pleasure from waxing lyrical about capital accumulation and the evils of 'making money from money.' Perhaps, likewise, there is many a rapacious capitalist who equally almost sound poetic (albeit in reverse) when bragging about the 'art' of making money. Maybe it would be better if money was viewed simply as a means to an end, not a great evil regardless or a goal solely in itself – either way, not really very poetic is it?

Friday 11th February

Still trying my best to find some sort of tenuous link between money and poetry.

Perhaps poetry could be the new way forward for the diehard Marxists in bringing about their revolution. Rather than 'dictating to the proletariat' with an iron fist, there could be a new sensitive twenty-first century version which seeks to overthrow the system with 'poetic revelations' about the corrupting power of money. Maybe that's what some of more colourful and peaceful anti-globalisation protestors are already attempting in the guise of their dissent through art. I'm guessing though that any diehard Marxists would probably view such actions as idealistic claptrap.

Saturday 12th February

Although paying the full room price for the night, we have another middle aged couple check-in who only stay in the room for a few hours.

'We have just driven over from our holiday home in France. All we want is to have a shower and sleep for a few hours before driving back to our home in Gloucestershire.'

Fairly expensive sleep and shower really, considering that they arrived at 11.30am and left around 1.30pm, but I guess if you've got the money what does it matter?

Sunday 13th February

A woman with her twelve year old daughter said goodbye to us in the dining room as she was checking out after three night's accommodation. We thanked her for choosing us and remarked that "we hope you have enjoyed your stay."

"Oh yes," she announced loudly whilst turning also to address all the other guests still having their breakfast. "This place is wonderful. You should see the absolute dive that my friends have been at the last few days. A right fleapit in comparison to here and, unbelievably, the rate was a lot more expensive there as well."

Nice that the stay was enjoyed but I'm not sure the other guests quite wanted to hear about 'fleapits' whilst eating breakfast? And should our prices be higher to reflect the deluxe non-flea environment?

Monday 14th February

Ok, perhaps it is a bit intrusive and unethical, but I'm sure many others would also take a quick peek inside a Valentines card if it was left out on display, especially if it was a big, soppy, red one. The only problem, however, after reading the message sent by our guest to his girlfriend is how to keep a straight face next time I bump into them both - the romantic devil had addressed the card, 'To Minge Muffin.'

Tuesday 15th February

It has happened so many times now that I assume it must be the normal telephone custom in France. Whenever French people phone up to make an enquiry they normally start the conversation by announcing (hear the comedy stereotypical accent to yourself), 'Allo, I am French.'

I am now always tempted to counter their grand opening with the reply, 'Allo, I am English.' Followed by, of course, 'but I shall say this only once.'

Wednesday 16th February

Just for the record, in case anyone is really interested in cross-cultural comparisons of different telephone customs, German-speaking people normally start their telephone conversations by announcing their first name and surname and then giving their full telephone number.

Thursday 17th February

Whilst servicing one of the rooms this morning I accidentally vacuumed up a pair of girl's knickers, which made a rather strange sound as it went up the hose. Luckily, the (bagless) cylinder was not very full and I was able to recover the knickers and just dust them down a bit before replacing them on the floor as if nothing had happened. Apologies if these were your knickers but, honestly, it was a genuine accident. Normally any knickers left on the floor would always be left in peace.

Friday 18th February

'Hello. We've just arrived in Brighton and have a booking with you but need directions and your address?'

It's amazing the amount of people who phone up just ahead of check-in who have no idea of the location. Why risk potentially losing your holiday because you haven't made a note of your booking? Or am I just pedantic in *always* having the full address and a map printed out whenever I stay somewhere?

Saturday 19th February

When guests are dressed head-to-toe in the full regalia of punk fashion - brightly coloured mohicans, tattoos, multiple piercing/pins, etc – it is more comforting if they are in the mould of Dom Jolly's character from *Trigger Happy TV* rather than types bent on anarchist destruction.

'Brighton has a wonderfully rich architectural history. Such aesthetic appeal. We just adore strolling along the seafront and absorbing the Regency splendour. Architecture is so profoundly important - an integral part of the cultural fabric.'

Maybe some punks have always been overly polite and intellectual, reveling in maximising the dichotomy between the expectations and behaviour of their appearance? The only thing missing from this couple, compared to the *Trigger Happy* punks, was the 'Fuck Off' written across their foreheads.

Our punk guests reveled additionally this morning when left alone in the dining room to make conversation with a rather startled and nervous looking elderly couple.

'Such lovely weather recently,' the punk man said. 'My wife and I find the coastal air so invigorating. A fresh wind, breathing in deeply the ions from the sea - good for the body and soul don't you think? … Are you here on holiday? … Well it's been smashing talking to you; hope you have a super day.'

Sunday 20th February

No big deal? Outrageously tactless? Inexcusable mistake? Is it a great *faux pas* to serve a full cooked breakfast (bacon, sausages and black pudding inclusive) to a vegetarian – especially if you've returned to the kitchen before realising the blunder?

If not offensive then maybe it would be polite to not stare blankly at the plate in muted silence when a B&B owner returns sheepishly to apologise? Or not maintain a pointedly stony exterior throughout eating the 'correct' vegetarian breakfast?

Perhaps though there is no real carnivore/vegetarian tension, solely another case of English reserve? Embarrassment and awkwardness, compounded further by a nervous desire to not cause a scene of any type. If the mistake had not been amended, the said vegetarian would probably have just helped themselves to some cereal and left the cooked breakfast aside without any complaint.

Monday 21st February

Can the mere cultural interpretation of a rainbow have any greater significance and meaning? We have a Nigerian academic staying with us this week attending a conference at the University of Sussex. I was standing on the step outside the B&B this afternoon, looking up at a vivid and beautifully coloured rainbow, when the Nigerian guy walked up the street.

'There must be a large pot of gold at the end of that one,' I casually remarked as he approached.

'You know in Africa, instead of a pot of gold, we say that there is a lion cub being born at the end of the rainbow,' he replied.

Could this juxtaposition perhaps be an interesting metaphor to describe the differences between Western and African civilization? Or is it no more than a simple contrast of fairy tales? Does African culture have its own version of *El Dorado* somewhere, just not at the end of a rainbow? And, if not, does it mean anything?

Tuesday 22nd February

Men, be warned! Some subjects, such as the female body clock and/or being compared to a younger woman, are potentially sensitive areas for your partner. Two couples have come away together for a few days, three of them in their thirties but with one of the women a bit younger. This morning I overheard a conversation regarding the recent engagement of the 'older' couple.

'It's absolutely amazing the amount of time and effort involved when you start to plan a wedding, not to mention the cost of course, but it feels like the right thing to do now at this stage of our relationship. We're really excited,' the older woman said.

'Yes,' replied her fiancé. 'It's definitely the right time. You think, by the time we actually tie the knot, Jo is going to be nearly thirty-three. And if you factor in that it may take a while to conceive we could be leaving things quite late if we want to start a family.'

'Alright darling. Don't panic too much. I've got plenty of time yet before my sell-by-date,' Jo replied.

'I know, but it's ok for these two with Sarah only being twenty-five. We've got to think about these things now,' the silver-tongued fiancé responded.

'Alright, I don't really need to be so publicly reminded of my age, thank you.'

Wednesday 23rd February

A couple in their forties, well dressed and affluent looking, were having breakfast this morning with their ten year old daughter. As I was clearing away another table with a number of other guests still in the dining room, the young daughter suddenly could be heard quite audibly.

'But mummy, what exactly are the working classes?' she clearly stated in very clipped tones.

The question, combined with catching the eye of another guest chuckling to himself, almost prompted me to break into a 'chipper' song and dance routine as I cleaned the table. Sadly, though, the temptation to give a spontaneous living educational example was resisted.

Thursday 24th February

Our next door neighbour rung on the doorbell at 2am. My first thoughts when I saw him were 'great - what problem do we have now' and I was actually relieved when he told me that he had locked himself out of his house.

'Sorry to trouble you but it's absolutely freezing out here and cloth ears [his partner] won't answer the door-bell. I've been ringing it now for about forty minutes - banging on the door and windows below as well and I just can't seem to wake him. Do you mind if I borrow your telephone to see if that works?'

Of course, being the good neighbour, I allowed him use our phone but did think to myself 'surely you could just have reversed the charges from the phone boxes opposite rather than wake us up as well?'

When there was no answer also from the phone I did offer him our sofa to sleep on (all our bedrooms were let for the night) but he declined and said 'he would just keep trying the bell until he gets through.'

'Ok. But just give us another ring if you're completely stranded. Our sofa will be better than sleeping on the beach and dying of hypothermia.'

Friday 25th February

I answered the doorbell again to my neighbour (at a more civilised hour of the day) only this time he was holding a huge bouquet of flowers.

'I'm ever so sorry for last night. It's all very embar-rassing. I did eventually get in but I hope these [the flow-ers] make up for you being disturbed.'

Especially as they were a very fragrant and expensive looking bouquet it probably more than compensated for merely offering help to a neighbour in distress.

Saturday 26th February

1.30am in the morning the bell goes again, only this time because some guests can't get in the front door. A previ-ous guest, either accidentally or on purpose, had knocked the latch down from the inside so blocking the door being opened. The guests stuck on the outside were understanding but I was less happy about getting woken up for the second time in three nights and going up to the door in my dressing gown.

Sunday 27th February

Now this is really becoming very annoying. 2am this morning the doorbell goes yet another time and I answer the door to a drunk and smelly guy asking whether we have any single rooms for the night. The answer, to put it politely, was 'no.'

Monday 28th February

For those of you who have never spent the majority of your time at home, it's quite astonishing just how many unsolicited sales calls you have to answer each daytime. Even more annoying, especially when you are extremely busy, is the unrelenting *sales script* persistence in not taking 'no' for an answer. It doesn't help, of course, that usually you also have to listen to a crackly three second overseas connection delay to then be lied to by a broad Indian accent announcing, 'Hello, my name is John Smith.' Still, can't help feeling sorry for these people really. They are only doing a job and earning a relative pittance. Most of us, after all, would not want to work sixty hours a week, for a few pence an hour, cold calling rich Indians pretending to be 'Rajiv Patel.'

MARCH

"Axe-wielding, medicated,
psycho nutter?"

Tuesday 1st March

Even though we are based in the 'gay village' of Kemp Town in Brighton (or Camp Town as it is sometimes known alternatively) over 95% of our guests are heterosexual. Granted we do not advertise specifically on any of the gay-only advertising websites but, surely, a city with the reputation of Brighton would attract an above average number of gay tourists? Or maybe because so many gays are already living here there is no need to visit as a tourist? Or perhaps we personally are just not targeting the 'pink pound' well enough?

The new exclusively male gay-only hotel next door has also been struggling with business and their vacancy sign shows in the window twenty-four/seven. Most of the neighbour's trade furthermore appears to be heterosexual couples and quite often hen parties which most other small hotels/B&Bs would refuse to take. Perhaps this is not surprising however? Not only are our neighbour's target audience *exclusively* gay (5% of the population); they are also male-only (2.5% of the population); and additionally a bondage establishment (which even if it encompasses 40% of gay men reduces the target population down to 1% of the total). Furthermore they also serve vegetarian breakfasts only! Given that only one in ten people are vegetarians the target audience of our *exclusive* neighbours - i.e gay vegetarian men into bondage - would be about 0.1% of the total population.

Wednesday 2nd March

Went into a room to change it this morning after a check out and was delighted to find a whole stack of toe nail clippings left in a pile on one of the bedside cabinets. Nice.

Thursday 3rd March

We are fully booked for a few days with Liberal Democrats who are in Brighton for a mini conference. Recently the political party has been going through a difficult patch with the leader resigning because of alcohol problems and also a senior party member, married with kids, resigning because of revelations about an affair with a homosexual prostitute. Being supposed easy-going 'liberal' types, who should be able to see the funny side of a joke, I was tempted to make an announcement at breakfast this morning.

'Welcome to our B&B and we hope you enjoy your stay with us. Just remember, though, no excessive drinking and please do not bring any rent boys back later.'

Probably best I refrained - people's sense of humour can be easily misjudged.

Friday 4th March

Talking of liberals and alcohol problems I have been wondering whether I am kidding myself about my own alcohol intake? I drink an average of around forty units of alcohol a week when the 'recommended' maximum intake for a man is between twenty-one and twenty-eight units. My theory, however, is that everybody lies to their doctors when asked about drinking habits so the safe health levels are wrongly distorted downwards - I tell my doctor for instance that I drink about twenty-five units. Therefore, if everyone else is as deceitful as me, the medical records should actually correlate to forty units being in the 'safe' zone? Nothing like distorted logic to justify another drink. Excellent. I'll pour myself another large glass of red.

Saturday 5th March

There is another one of the many London to Brighton rallies this weekend which has seen the city invaded this time by hordes of mainly middle aged men on mopeds and scooters. There are quite a few younger people as well but the main theme of the rally is a celebration of the Mods from the 1960's. Many of the bikes are collector piece originals from the era and a lot of others are souped-up modern versions. When I told my dad about the rally he recounted his own Mod past and how, replete with the full length green parka and other regalia, he came down to Brighton in the sixties to fight the Rockers on the beach.

Apparently, though, the local police were having none of it and forced them all to dismount their bikes, push them to the edge of town, and then ride off back to London before any trouble could start. Don't fight with the law hey – they normally win!

Sunday 6th March

We describe the traditional fry-up option on our breakfast menu as an 'English Breakfast.' For the last four days, though, we have had a Japanese couple in who insist on upgrading our fry-up to a more 'supranational' cuisine.

'Could we have two *British* breakfasts, please,' they always announce proudly whilst beaming smiles at us.

Perhaps in some sort of Unionist spirit we should rename it to 'British Breakfast,' but doesn't quite sound right really? Although I'm sure, from a *cuisine* point of view anyway, there is not too much difference between English, Scottish, Welsh or (Northern) Irish fry-ups.

Monday 7th March

Perhaps it's just a coincidence (or maybe the Scandinavian countries coordinate their holidays together?) but we have separate guest bookings staying at the moment from Denmark, Sweden and Norway. With the usual oxymoronic caveat of being suspicious of stereotypes whilst then also constantly observing them, we tend to find Scandinavians to be very well behaved and pleasant guests. A Spanish teacher, at a language school in Malaga a few years back, always used to make fun of our fellow Scandinavian students by saying they 'had ice in the in their veins' - in unfavourable contrast, of course, to the (supposed) feisty and colourful Latin temperament. If nationalities though do have stereotypical personalities is geography or politics the greater determining factor? Are Scandinavians such a 'cool' and 'sensible' bunch because of the cold, dark climate and relatively sparse population or more a direct result of social democratic harmony? And if the harmonious Nordic politics of being wealthy, educated, ecologically minded and egalitarian is mainly what creates a level-headed character then what are the implications? Is a future utopia for the planet going to end up being a bit dull?

Tuesday 8th March

Football grounds in England are apparently losing some of their atmosphere because the growing middle class audience is not as passionate as the 'jolly' working classes which used to dominate. Surely the same conundrum as the Scandinavian question yesterday? If only middle class people could just experience a degree of misery from time to time then perhaps the excitement of a 'fiery' temperament would not be lost. Maybe some sort of *smorgasbord* package; nothing too intense, where you could purchase different types of short-term misery 'injections' would be sufficient - day trips around the *favelas*, an evening out with tramps etc. Mind you, fiery temperaments and personalities are not necessarily all that desirable. And lets not forget also, in relation to those Scandinavians, the culture of naked saunas and sexual liberation - a riposte surely to accusations of being dull. No, the truth really is that misery is a bit overrated these days.

Wednesday 9th March

It's a good warning of potential trouble if guests are already slightly tipsy when they check-in. At 11pm we heard a loud banging from upstairs and I went up to discover a young lesbian couple that arrived earlier now extremely drunk and stumbling around in the porch.

'Have you double-locked the door so we can't get in,' they belligerently said, as two bottles of wine in a carrier bag banged heavily against the wall as they swayed.

'No, maybe you're just too drunk. And I would prefer to not have my door barged into and the whole house woken up.'

'This is Brighton man - anything goes. We can do what we want.'

'Well perhaps you're not in a fit state to stay as a guest in my house.'

One of the young women at this point released a whole torrent of screaming obscenities which gave me no choice but to take the key and tell them to leave. Eventually, following a lot more loud abuse, both finally left after I threatened to call the police. It may be 'liberal' Brighton but it doesn't mean you have to put up with paralytic drunks vandalising your house and being aggressive.

Thursday 10th March

'Bloody cigarette smoke,' I cursed under my breath leaving a bedroom but not realising another guest was in the corridor.

'Sorry. Ignore my grumblings. It's just a particular bugbear which always infuriates us.'

'No, don't you worry. It's perfectly understandable. It's a disgusting habit and if someone done that in my house I'd be damn annoyed as well,' the female guest sympathetically replied.

'It just takes ages to get rid of the smell from every-where. I'm not sure smokers realise sometimes exactly how much cigarette smoke stinks. Too used to the smell maybe being constantly with them? Or don't care either way? Not to mention the fire risk,' I carried on, unable to stop moaning.

'I can tell you of a good remedy for getting rid of cigarette smell actually. I read it in a women's magazine once. Apparently if you leave a plate of salt in the room it's supposed to soak up all the smell of the smoke.'

Not sure whether it will work but worth a go. Maybe I should spend more time reading women's magazines.

Friday 11ᵗʰ March

George W. Bush has just announced a $400 billion share dividend tax cut which will overwhelmingly benefit the richest 1% of Americans only - the three million people least in the world who need some extra money (and coin-cidentally also including Bush and his chums?) The same money could give $10,000 of health insurance a year to each of the forty million Americans who do not have any medical cover. Or provide the ten million unemployed Americans with jobs paying $40,000 a year each. Or, if really daring, double the annual income of the one billion people worldwide who live on a dollar a day. Still, I guess those richest three million need the tax cut if incentives are to be maintained - not being able to afford that second private jet is bound to impact on where best to invest your share portfolio?

Saturday 12th March

We have a couple of Japanese girls with us who are visiting Brighton whilst studying in London for the past year. Although they speak English very well I find myself feeling slightly deflated when talking to them because their native accent has been completely subsumed by the new hybrid accent that is developing amongst foreign students/workers who have been living here (specifically in London) a long time. Great, of course, that the world is becoming fluently bi-lingual so that we can all communicate well with each other. I just wish the endearing Oriental twang or the sensual French 'va va vroom' could be retained a bit more instead of being replaced with an 'innit' London accent.

Sunday 13th March

Some men can be real romantic charmers.

'Hello,' a woman in her late twenties had said on Friday when checking-in alone for a two night booking. 'My boyfriend couldn't make it to Brighton at the same time so it's just me for now. Hopefully I'm going to rendezvous with him at some point later.'

Obviously they did eventually meet up because both were together at breakfast this morning. However, despite the continuing attempts by the woman at being bright and breezy, there was a distinct awkwardness in the air as her boyfriend's muted persona clearly indicated he was bored and disinterested.

Servicing the rooms later we bumped into the woman leaving the house alone.

'Just going out to have a look at the shops,' she said. 'Oh, and you don't have to worry though about cleaning our room. My boyfriend is being lazy and has gone back to bed. Sorry to be a pain.'

'That's ok. No need to apologise. You're entitled to a lie-in when on holiday,' I replied cheerfully but thinking it would perhaps be a bit more romantic to be in bed or go out sightseeing/shopping together.

About five minutes later the TV from their room was put on and *Football Focus* started blaring out loudly - obviously the boyfriend had quickly woken up from his holiday snooze! The TV then also remained on loudly for the rest of the afternoon.

The 'romance' continued today when the woman appeared alone again at breakfast in a room full of other happy couples.

'Just a table for one please. My boyfriend says he's not in the mood for any food this morning.'

On check-out the fantastic weekend away was then topped off when the woman paid for the entire stay on her credit card while miserable mute boyfriend stood looking gormlessly on. Maybe *Mr. Amour* has some hidden qualities only she knows about?

Monday 14th March

Helen was being served today in one of our local fruit and veg stores which is run by an Egyptian family.

'Are you Scottish?' the man serving her suddenly asked.

'No.'

'Well you look like one.'

Surely it is a rather sweeping generalization to immediately assume anyone with red hair is from Scotland, even if the country does have the highest percentage of red-haired people in the world? The red gene, after all, has been spread far and wide across the globe by adventurous scarlet-headed breeders. Has our shopkeeper friend actually been to Scotland? Plenty of blondes, brunettes and black-haired people last time I was there.

It's not the first time though that Helen's hair colour has attracted such interest. On a family holiday in Scotland as children, Helen and her younger brother were mobbed one time by Japanese tourists. Quietly minding their own business at a picturesque vista lookout the children suddenly attracted the fevered attention of a coach load of Japanese tourists who pulled up. Rather than be interested in the countryside view the Japanese were more concerned about taking pictures of the flame-haired children as if both were part of some Scottish theme park.

By the way - is it just a coincidence that Scottish Highland cattle also have red hair? Or is there something about the Scottish/Celtic landscape that leads to the evolution of the red gene?

Tuesday 15th March

An older couple in their seventies checked-out today after a three day holiday with us.

'I've paid a one night deposit but I still owe you the money for the other two days,' the man said as they brought their bags slowly down the stairs on departure.

'Don't worry - I didn't think you were the types to do a runner on us,' I replied, innocently referring to the fact that they seemed such nice (and hence) trustworthy people.

'Yes, I guess you're right. Our bones are probably a bit rickety to make a quick enough getaway from you.'

Not sure whether the couple had misinterpreted my comment and was slightly offended or were just joking back? Either way, does that make me or them more self-conscious about their age?

Wednesday 16ᵗʰ March

Another uplifting conversation with my dad today about running the B&B.

'Yeh, I think it's all settling down quite nicely now actually. Working out a lot better than we expected,' I said in a reasonably upbeat tone.

'Mmm, I guess. Just still seems a shame to be wasting your thirties doing it. This is your prime - you should be making the most of it really.'

What decade of a man's life constitutes his prime anyhow? Sexual peak/prime is in the teenage years, sporting/athletic prime is in the twenties, money-making prime in the forties/fifties, and intellectual prime in the sixties perhaps or even seventies. Maybe if you combine all of these different peaks together you could somehow argue the thirties are your best years but who wants to celebrate the decade of being average? Regardless, if you define yourself as 'past it' at any point in your life, you're inevitably on a losing wicket, always mourning the 'lost' glory years. Why bother looking back or forward comparatively, be happy wherever you are?

And 'wasting' my life? That's a real positive, uplifting boost to the ego. Or being *Zen* should such matters not be of concern – the ego being transcended? Perhaps the real lesson here is the highlighting of psychological undertones – maybe perversely the main driving force behind this writing.

Thursday 17th March

Amazing how people come away on holiday, yet still feel the need to share their *grumpy old gitishness* with you.

'The trouble these days is that people don't want to work. There are so many benefits now that everyone thinks they can sit around doing nothing and scrounge off the state. It's us hardworking taxpayers though that foots the bill. It's all wrong. The world's gone mad.'

Normal good practice, of course, would be to make your guests feel comfortable and happy regardless (and perhaps especially so given that we were honoured to be co-identified as such decent fellow tax-paying citizens.) And maybe a good-natured quip to appease our guests and satisfy some shared sense of indignation would have been easier. However, these two were plain irksome and a conciliatory mood did not seem appropriate.

'Maybe true for some,' I replied, 'but I think most people actually want to work.'

'Hmm,' was the response, slightly taken aback that an assumed consensus outlook was being challenged before just continuing as before. 'The trouble is really that bene-fits are too high so people have no incentive to go to work.'

'Why does the unemployment level vary so much at different times then? In the 1930s, early 80s, early 90s, and the credit crunch now, is it just a coincidence that an extra three million people become unemployed? Do people suddenly become lazy dole scroungers in these periods or is something else weird happening such as severe economic recession?'

After a rather strained silence and bewildered frowns the couple quickly excused themselves to 'get ready' for the day. When we later serviced their room there was a copy of Middle England's favourite newspaper on the table. Would such reading matter have any bearing on an outlook that views people and the world in an overly cynical fashion?

Friday 18th March

Inviting strangers to stay overnight in your house inevitably has a certain amount of behavioural risk asso-ciated with it. Given this fact, financial need notwith-standing, it is obviously wise to try and obviate the associated risks as much as possible. Perhaps, though, despite some of the less savoury incidents that have previously occurred, we have now taken this expediency a little too much to heart?

Firstly we have now stopped turning the window vacancy signs. This avoids the less organised 'on the day' trade and especially the drunks who come to the door looking for a room.

Secondly, we have started to actively discriminate against anyone on the phone who sounds even slightly dodgy by telling them we are fully booked even if rooms are available. Snobby, maybe, but you can predict with uncanny accuracy exactly how someone will behave just from their telephone voice and manner. If they sound like an idiot, they will probably behave like an idiot and it is not worth the risk.

Thirdly, we never accept Hen and Stag groups, now extended to any single sex group larger than two, especially if they are men. As Tubbs said in *The League of Gentlemen* 'they come in groups of ones and twos' and that is far too many for our liking.

And, fourthly, we have now started to check people's email addresses after spotting an inquiry from someone going by the name of 'psychobitch@ .....co.uk.' (does this person use the same email address on their CV when making a job application?) Other endearing email address names which have been discarded are: 'Prozac_depressive@ ....co.uk,' 'ravingnutter@ ....co.uk' and 'axewielder@ ....co.uk.'

It's not that snobby, surely, to not want axe wielding, medicated depressive, psycho nutters to stay in your house is it? Apart from if they are family of course.

Saturday 19th March

Talking about strange guests, we had a bizarre woman in her early forties stay with us last night. She drove down from Birmingham but phoned a number of times on the way to explain that she would be arriving late because she kept 'losing' her way. When she actually arrived in

Brighton we received another three flustered calls asking the same repeated questions about our exact location and parking.

'Sorry for being so late,' she said after finally arriving, 'I never drive on motorways. I don't trust them at all. Always think I'll go the wrong way down them and end up in the opposite end of the country. Everyone drives too fast as well. Too scary. Got lost anyway trying to find my way down all the small roads. It's taken me forever to get here. I've been going round in circles.'

This morning she then turned up for breakfast looking rather harassed and rubbing her arms with shivers.

'I've had a really terrible night. You'll never guess what's happened to me. I've been stuck outside in my car since five this morning because I lost my keys. It's absolutely freezing out there.'

'Oh no,' I replied, assuming she had lost the front door/room keys. 'There was no need to have stayed outside. You should have just rung on the doorbell and we would have let you back in.'

'No, no. I have my hotel keys. Look,' she said holding them up for me to see. 'As I was getting out of my car yesterday evening my car keys fell out of my lap and went straight down the drain. My breakdown cover people said they would get to me first thing in the morning to sort it out so I got up early to wait for them. They haven't arrived yet so can I just grab some breakfast quickly?'

'Of course. Did the breakdown people not give you a more specific time though? Surely they don't expect you to wait through the night for them?'

'Well, they did say it would be first thing sometime after 7am but I didn't want to miss them in case they turned up early.'

Despite her anxiety (or should that be neurosis) to not miss her breakdown service it did not prevent the woman from then talking non-stop to myself and the other two couples already in the dining room.

'Dear me, dear me. Why do things like this always happen to me? On holiday as well. I've only come away for a few days break and my car keys go down the drain like that. They should be able to replace it mind. That's what they told me ......' and so she went on as I returned to the kitchen to leave our other guests quietly listening.

The woman then, and obviously assuming that other people wanted to continue listening to her, started on a prejudiced rant.

'It's pretty scary as well being out there all alone at five in the morning. Very dark and not many people around. And it's inner city here as well. That makes things more dangerous. I'm not racist but I get scared when I see black people around. I don't like it at home either but more so here because I'm not familiar with this area. My grand-child is black mind, although that doesn't make any difference to me, I still find them all threatening.'

Where to start hey? Not wanting to drive on motor-ways and being bad at navigation - not the greatest crime. Sitting out in a freezing car through the night for no reason - slightly barking mad. Racist and prejudiced, even though your own grandchild is mixed race - sad.

Sunday 20ᵗʰ March

A man from London, around forty years old, is in a room by himself after previously staying here for a weekend break with his partner a few months ago. When I ask him why he is back in town he is quite open about the reason despite the potential criminal nature of his visit.

'Well last time I was down here with the missus some bouncer cracked me right on the chin and did some pretty serious damage. The police won't press charges though so I'm going to take things into my own hands. I've followed where he lives. I know where he goes to the gym. And I've been phoning to put the "shit" up him a bit. He says he ain't scared but I'm not leaving it - going to make sure that I'm on his mind.'

Don't know what else was planned for his bouncer foe but he will be returning again next month apparently to 'continue' with him.

Monday 21st March

An actor is staying with us for a week whilst performing at the Theatre Royal and gave us two complimentary tickets today because we 'have been such nice hosts.' The job could be worse.

Tuesday 22nd March

It's probably nice when older people act like they want to adopt you? A German couple, we think partly due to the fact that Helen is apparently the spitting image of their daughter-in-law, have been acting extremely affectionate towards us. This affection reached a climax at breakfast this morning when they were saying goodbye just before checking out.

'We have loved our stay here and we love you two,' the woman said in a heavy accent as her husband smiled broadly on. 'We so love this building and this house. The rooms are so lovely as well. We have had such a good holiday. It has been wonderful. We love you. You remind us so much of our son's wife. We love you. Thank you. Thank you. Goodbye. We love you.'

As we abashedly wished them all the best in return, pleased, but slightly taken aback by the outpouring of emotion, I caught the eye of the only other guest in the dining room at the time - a young man in his mid-twenties.

'That was a bit gushing,' he said with droll under-statement.

'Don't worry,' I replied, 'We don't expect all our guests to proclaim their love for us when they leave.'

Wednesday 23rd March

A couple from Leeds were walking down the stairs, not realising I'm in the hallway, and the man was having hysterics of laughter.

'Having a good time?' I asked when they spotted me.

'Oh yes. I just managed to get a fart out right on my girlfriend. We have a great relationship with each other, we do.'

'Yep, certainly seems so.'

Not sure the girlfriend was thinking the same though?

Thursday 24th March

Every so often we get requests for no deposit money to be taken in advance from credit/debit cards because people would prefer to pay in cash. We usually assume, cynical as it may, that (self-employed) people are trying to 'lose' some cash to avoid paying tax. Today we had another such 'prefer to pay in cash' request only this time on behalf of a church group attending a conference in Brighton. Now, of course, this could be a completely innocent request unconnected to any tax evasion matters. Surely it is more interesting however to believe the church organisation is just as dodgy as many of the wider public flock. Or is tax dodging not really immoral because tax more represents 'government theft' than 'worthy' public spending?

Friday 25th March

'It smells of cigarette smoke in the corridor so I'm just reminding you that we are a non-smoking establishment,' I had warned a middle aged English couple two days ago (although they flatly denied they had been smoking.)

Yesterday we had seen from our backyard that the same couple's room had its window fully open despite it being a cold day. When we later serviced the room there was a strong musty smell notwithstanding the cold fresh air blasting in from the still fully open window. That evening we once more could smell cigarette smoke in the corridor.

'Look we know you are smoking. Please could you not smoke in the house or I will have to ask you to leave,' I told them.

'It's not from here,' they repeated once more, completely straight faced. 'We haven't been smoking at all. You've got the wrong room. Honest. Try the room next door.'

When someone so confidently and assertively stands their ground it does make you wonder slightly whether your own facts are straight, but we knew for sure the other room were not smokers (and had already unfairly disturbed them before in checking).

'If I smell anymore smoke in this house someone is going to be leaving early,' was my curt reply.

This morning, after the 'denial' couple had checked out, we found two empty packets of cigarettes along with the same accompanying musty smell of cigarette smoke. Also in the room was a large empty gift box from a 'Government Warnings Suck' novelty present range. The message on the gift read, in bold letters; 'Smoking is my Choice. So Fuck off.'

Saturday 26th March

Our local pub has a big chalkboard outside which says 'Free Pool on Tuesdays.' As I was walking past it today on the way to the supermarket for provisions I noticed that some wag had rubbed off the letter 'l' from the word 'pool.' I won't be recommending the new free food menu to guests.

Sunday 27th March

There was a London to Brighton cycle ride yesterday and we have four cyclists in who completed the trip together.

'Sorry to bother you,' one of them said to me at breakfast this morning whilst the other three were in fits of giggles. 'But I was just passing my friend a tomato from my plate when it fell off my fork into his tea. You couldn't possibly bring us another pot could you?'

'Of course,' I replied looking down at the floating tomato. 'You should have just said though if you prefer tomatoes cooked in this way. We'll put it formally on the menu so you can choose it in advance next time you stay.'

Later on I overheard one of them talking about a safari holiday he had been on this year.

'Do you know the most dangerous animal for tourists in Africa - the one that kills far more than any other animal - is the hippo, not any of the big cats or crocodiles or elephants or snakes.'

'Oh I would never have guessed that,' his friend responded, 'especially as hippos are vegetarians aren't they?'

'Animals can't be vegetarians you idiot,' another replied to more laughter. 'They're herbivores - they don't choose to not eat meat because of their ethical concern for the world.'

Or perhaps the potential ethical concern of these herbivore animals could just be a case of 'hippie' politics.

Monday 28th March

An air hostess from Detroit has brought her thirteen year old daughter with her for a brief holiday in England in between working transatlantic shifts. For all those convinced that 'England is going to the dogs' and want to leave the country a few conversations with this woman may well change minds. A sort of American version of Harry Enfield's comedy German character that always has to 'apologise for the war,' only for her it is US foreign policy and general cultural malaise that needs the repentance.

'It's just so terrible what's happening in the States at the moment,' she volunteered to me again at breakfast this morning. 'Bush has just been a complete disaster. It's so embarrassing now going abroad all the time when you are an American. You feel you have to actively distance yourself from your country's policies and our idiot leader and apologise all the time. He [Bush] is just such a jerk. Denying climate change and refusing to sign Kyoto. The absolute mess of Iraq. Guantanamo bay. I'm ashamed to be an American at the moment.'

'Well Britain and quite a few other countries have been involved in Iraq as well,' I replied trying to blunt slightly the unremitting anti-American sentiment.

'Yeh, but we all know it was Bush and his lot that twisted everybody's arms into it. You know not all of us [Americans] are now eating Freedom Fries and calling the French "cheese eating surrender monkeys." There are a lot of good folks back home too that care and think things are going very wrong. Mind you where I live at the moment it is pretty bad. There are lots of murders happening and drugs. I'd like to move out to the country somewhere or I would move over here if I could. I love England. The people are so nice and re-laxed and friendly. And seem so intelligent. And the countryside is so beautiful.'

So there you go. Think carefully anyone planning to emigrate. England is officially a green and pleasant utopia - a litter-free paradise populated only by laid back, pleasant and educated people. That's right isn't it?

Tuesday 29th March

A leisurely day reading on the beach would be a lot more relaxing if we didn't have guests in the house to phone our mobile.

'Hello. Is that Scott? It's Kim and Tania calling from room five. Sorry to trouble you but there is water dripping down through the ceiling and light fittings. I think someone has left a tap on upstairs but they are not answering their door.'

'Ok. Thanks for letting us know. We're only a couple of minutes away so we'll be back very soon,' I replied, my tranquil state truncated abruptly.

When we returned we found twin beds pushed apart and towels on the floor to soak up a steady drip of water that was coming through the light fittings. There was also a large wet patch spreading across to one of the walls where water was additionally trickling down. Immediately running upstairs we indeed found the occupants out and the tap left on to about three-quarters pressure. The en suite bathroom floor was absolutely flooded and the water had also heavily soaked out into most of the room carpet. Once again the culprit, leaving aside any irresponsibility of leaving a tap running, was our electric macerator toilet. The fuse had eventually blown which meant the water flowed up and out of the toilet rather than being pumped away – yes, delightful.

'We've found the source of the water and shut it off,' I told the young women below. 'Apologies for the inconvenience. Your room should be ok now and these water stains should dry out. I can arrange another B&B if the stains detract too much from your stay?'

ZEN AND THE DIARY OF A B&B OWNER

'No, it's fine. We don't mind so long as it's fixed. Is it safe to turn the lights on though with all that water?'

'Oh yes,' I replied, hoping to not be electrocuted as I flicked the switch to demonstrate.

I then rushed downstairs to grab as many old towels as possible to soak up the main flooded room. Incredibly, just as I reached the outside store cupboard, another seagull decided to have an apoplectic seizure whilst flying overhead. Out of nowhere a whistling downdraft almost grazed my head as the thud of a semi-comatose seagull landed on the ground next to me. What are the odds?

The strange seagull being the lesser of my immediate concerns, I returned quickly upstairs to face hours of tedious soaking up of water. The room, despite a couple of heaters and much use of a water suction carpet machine, was still saturated by the time the couple who had left the tap running eventually got back. We didn't have any major altercation and the couple were very remorseful and volunteered to forgo the rest of their stay. However who is going to pay if we can't re-let this room for some considerable time while it is drying out, and for proper carpet cleaning and re-painting? Smelly, dank carpets, along with warped under boards are not the most luxurious B&B facilities people want. The seagull, still unable to fly, wasn't interested though when I told him.

Wednesday 30th March

Our neighbours had a young oriental couple stay with them yesterday who rang the internal doorbell at 4am, which is only supposed to be used during the night if there is an emergency.

'Do you have any condoms that we could have?' the young couple asked.

Not quite the emergency the neighbours normally expect to deal with, although they did suggest the 24 hour shop just around the corner as advice. It could have been a genuine desperate moment however. Perhaps it should be law that Hoteliers/B&B owners have to always be available to provide condoms - a sort of additional public health service to help prevent unwanted pregnancies and sexually transmitted diseases. Maybe they should give us the morning after pill as well to dispense in case there are no available chemists nearby?

Thursday 31st March

All the B&B is now fully en suite apart from one room which has a private bathroom situated just along the corridor. This afternoon, a few hours after checking into a normal en suite room, a woman was standing outside the private bathroom in the corridor looking like she was about to wet herself.

'You don't know if anyone is definitely in this bathroom do you?' she asked whilst fidgeting uncomfortably from side to side. 'I've been waiting here for ages now and no one has come out.'

'Well this bathroom is private to room one just here.'

'What bathroom can I use then and how do I find it,' she replied perplexed and anxious.

'You booked a double en suite so you have a bathroom inside your own room.'

'Oh really. I never realised. I'll go and see if it's there.'

Two men who coincidentally are working on fitting signs in the Brighton Centre happened to also walk in at the same time as the conversation occurred.

'It's not that hard to find the en suites is it?' I questioned them.

'Well we never had any problems but we can do you some big signs to put on the doors if you want?'

APRIL

Launderette irony?

Friday 1ˢᵗ April

A few days ago we noticed an odd smell in one of the en suite bathrooms that appeared to be coming back through the extractor system. Not being able to work out the source to remedy the situation we decided to put an air freshener behind the toilet to mask the smell and ameliorate the problem temporarily. Yesterday we asked a German couple staying in the room if everything was ok.

'Yes the guest house and the room are lovely and we are really enjoying our visit. We had noticed though that the bathroom smells a bit,' they replied.

Blast, we thought, how are going to fix this one? We have no idea what's causing the smell. However, when we later serviced their room, the extractor system appeared to be working normally again and the bathroom had a pleasant 'alpine' freshness to it.

This morning at breakfast the German couple came down both beaming widely.

'It's ok,' they announced. 'We have found out the problem with the bathroom. It was this behind the toilet [handing me the air freshener we had put in]. We really do not like the smell it makes. It's terrible.'

Saturday 2ⁿᵈ April

'Ah, we may be able to understand and speak some of the language but we Swedes are not the same as other Scandinavians. We have a much better sense of humour,'

I was informed in a merry bit of neighbour baiting by some Swedish guests today. 'The Norwegians especially. When the comedy film *Life of Brian* was released in Sweden it was advertised as "so funny it is banned in Norway,"' they continued bursting into guffaws.

Sunday 3rd April

Sometimes you really do wonder what makes some people choose an obviously loathsome human being as a romantic partner. Why would a seemingly intelligent, attractive, good natured, professional woman in her thirties choose to date a rude, fat, obnoxious, ill-mannered, racist slob of the same age? It wasn't a question I did put to the particular couple whom I refer, but it would have been more than valid to do so.

When this couple arrived yesterday I took an instant dislike to the man who was conceited and arrogant in stark contrast to the friendly and pleasant manner of his partner. My view of this idiot further nose-dived when he returned drunk in the evening stomping up the stairs shouting.

'Whoaa, yeeee, whoa,' in a loud sort of football chant voice, 'I should have kicked that Paki's head in.'

'Excuse me,' I shouted after him as I quickly stormed out of the lounge into the hallway. 'Do you want to shut up? Do not use racist language in the first place in this house and don't disturb me and all the other guests either. You can leave right now otherwise.'

'Alright mate, alright. Calm down,' he spluttered after first sizing me up as if he was about to start a confrontation.

After this disagreeable incident the same man then came down to breakfast this morning all fat and sweaty and rather abruptly, especially considering the last time we spoke, demanded without any please to have 'a full English but with extra bacon and extra sausages.' I again looked at the woman with utter incomprehension as to why she was in a relationship with this man.

A few hours later this same unfathomable sentiment continued to an even greater degree when noisy sex could be overheard from their room. Clearly it was not desirable to have a mental picture of this fat, racist slob having sex but it was impossible to ignore as the most bizarre grunts and groans emanated loudly into the corridor. Then, just as I was shaking my head in disbelief going down the stairs, the 'slob' man and his girlfriend came in the front door. There was a turn - the pantomime sex noises were coming from the room next door which was let to a very skinny, introverted couple who have been all nervous and shy when making conversation. Perhaps it is true then what they say about the quiet ones?

Monday 4th April

Marcel, a German business traveller, is staying with us for a few weeks whilst working on computer systems at the nearby American Express head office. He is nearly fluent in English but, as ever with non-native language speakers, not quite 100% perfect. Yesterday he had asked where he could find a nearby launderette and whether a service wash was available.

'Did you get your washing sorted out ok?' I enquired to him this morning.

'Oh yes. I did thank you,' replied Marcel. 'There was no *irony* available at the launderette though.'

Guessing that he actually meant 'ironing' rather than commenting on the lack of dry humour from our local laundry service, Marcel was very amused when his mispronunciation was corrected.

Perhaps, however, there is a humour shortage at the launderette? If a visitor walks into your establishment and queries, 'Is there *irony* available here?' it must deserve a quip back surely. They could have responded, for instance; 'How about a no smoking sign up in a cigarette factory.'

Tuesday 5th April

Nobody is booked in for the next few days so we have decided to take advantage of the natural lull and take some time off, especially as we are already full for the coming weekend. Surely we deserve a break after working constantly for the last three months – it is supposed to be a lifestyle business?

Friday 8th April

'Don't worry, we're not the types to trash the room or anything,' a middle aged mum, staying with her grown-up daughter, said on arrival today.

'Oh, I'm not concerned at all. You both look very trustworthy.'

'Well she should be trustworthy,' the mum added. 'She's a police officer. Although she doesn't look like one, I know. Still a little baby.'

The daughter gave a wry grimace at this point, as if to say, 'Mum, I deal fine with all sorts of difficult situations and responsibilities in my job. I'm not a child anymore.'

Saturday 9th April

'We don't want to sleep the night, just have a shower and get changed,' a couple said today after running a local half-marathon.

'We do have a room but we only let rooms by the day, not by the hour.'

'No problem. We'll pay the full night rate. We just really want to freshen up.'

Within half an hour the key had been left and the couple had checked-out. There must be cheaper places surely if you are only after a shower? And we don't think it was a ruse either for a quick bit of hanky-panky because both were wearing tracksuits and the bed wasn't even sat on.

Sunday 10th April

A grumpy old man staying with his wife would not stop moaning yesterday because they would miss breakfast from leaving early, and that we don't stock enough tea supplies in the room - there are eight sachets each of tea and coffee provided every day.

'Should have been more in the room in the first place,' was his only response when we gave him an additional eight sachets of tea, and milk cartons.

This morning, after check out, we discover the whole complimentary basket emptied, including the coffee that the couple supposedly 'doesn't like.'

Monday 11th April

'Urggh. That's disgusting. Some of these carrots have gone mouldy. Urggh. They're all mushy and brown,' Helen shouted out, not realising I was on the phone in the dining room trying to take a booking.

Not really what you want the guests to overhear. We don't serve carrots for breakfast however - perhaps I should have let the guests booking a room know that?

Tuesday 12th April

We have a group of four guests who have arrived, two parents with their grown-up daughter and her boyfriend, all attending a 'Maharaji' conference at the Brighton Centre about 'peace and harmony.' Overhearing these guests talk about the conference at breakfast this morning I was intrigued to find out more about the Maharaji - a guru who seemed to offer a path to personal wisdom which ultimately could lead to the 'greater good of the whole planet' if only enough people were to 'take' this knowledge path.

'The Maharaji believes that if only everyone could find inner spiritual peace with themselves [through his unique "key" system] than all the world's problems would be solved,' one of them sincerely told me.

'And if you think about it really it is true,' another added with equal heartfelt belief. 'All the terrible things happening could easily be stopped if only enough people genuinely came to "peace" with themselves.'

As much as I quite liked all four of these people, who incidentally had found some sort of inner peace themselves because they were a cheerful good natured bunch, it was impossible to not respond slightly provocatively to such naïve idealism.

'It's a lot more difficult though to find "inner peace" when you're illiterate and semi-starving in some Third World shanty town.'

'Well, maybe,' was the reluctant reply after a few seconds thought, 'but the Maharaji still shows that we can all achieve peace within ourselves regardless of circumstances and this is the *key* for happiness.'

Surely it is a bit patronizing for affluent people with a good education (or even those fortunate enough to merely read and write given that a billion adults are illiterate worldwide) to assume that simply 'changing your inner thoughts' can solve all problems? Why worry about malnutrition, starvation, disease, shelter, lack of sanitation, when happiness is 'all in the mind?' The global poor are clearly not seeing the woods for the trees - happiness is obtainable if only they grasped it, just accepted their lot in life and be content.

Or perhaps the Maharaji's belief is that 'everyone finding their inner peace' could translate into a new politics whereby poverty, war, crime, climate change and all the other crises that exist will be surmounted by a transformed exigency? Good to have optimism of the will, granted, but democracy doesn't even exist in most of the world. And even if people were sufficiently educated enough and not preoccupied with basic survival to avail such democratic freedoms, would the choices necessary be made anyhow? There has to be a slight 'pessimism of the intellect' (to quote Gramsci) when you consider the reluctance of the rich to share even a miniscule increased percentage of their wealth.

Still, as a humble B&B owner merely serving breakfast, perhaps it was best to not have a full blown political remonstration with the guests. Such restraint, however, was additionally tested when the Maharaji's divinity was further espoused.

'And the great thing about the Maharaji is that you know he is genuine because he doesn't charge anything. As he says "how can I charge money when all knowledge is free?"'

'So it doesn't cost anything to see him speak or to buy his books and tapes?'

'Well it is free really, but he has to make some charge for expenses obviously. And when you obtain each of the six *keys* there is a shipping/handling charge. But we understand he has to cover costs - the important thing is that anyone can gain his knowledge.'

As I have never heard of the Maharaji before I did not want to add further cynicism by doubting his monetary intentions as well as his philosophy. And given that my guests were so personally content and invigorated perhaps his 'knowledge keys' do work? Despite their inner happiness, though, the 'all you need is love' mantra would not persuade me too much if I was poor and starving. A bit of money or a job would have to come first - the love bit can wait for later.

Wednesday 13th April

Talking of helping the poor and the hypocritical rich, who lecture about charity whilst siphoning money through offshore havens to avoid paying tax, a guest at breakfast this morning had a funny story about Bono. Apparently Bono was at a gig in Glasgow giving the usual harangue to lesser tax paying mortals - although I don't think he said anything about leading by example and giving up the jet set lifestyle and multiple homes? Anyway, as part of the lecture, Bono started to clap his hands to illustrate a point more forcibly only to be poleaxed by some quick-witted Glaswegian humour.

'Every time I clap my hands [whilst illustrating poignantly every second into the microphone] a child in Africa dies needlessly,' Bono recited.

'Well stop bloody doing it then,' shouted someone from the audience.

Thursday 14th April

A man phoned up today to question our booking policy. He had sent an email requesting information and prices for a double room and received a reply that read, 'sorry but we do not accommodate large groups.' Refraining from making the joke again about not accepting 'gangs of ones and twos' I apologised and explained that the wrong signature reply must have been accidentally sent.

Friday 15th April

We had the annual surprise inspection visit today from the AA to reassess our accommodation star rating.

Although slightly nervous about whether standards will be judged to the same level and our classification renewed, everything went fine and the inspector seemed impressed with our management and facilities. There was even a bonus when a corkscrew was spotted in one of the rooms which had actually been left by the previous guests and not cleared away as should have happened when the room was remade.

'I see you provide corkscrews for the guests as well. That's a nice additional touch that is appreciated by guests in terms of level of service. It's these small extra details that make all the difference,' the inspector informed us.

'Yes,' I replied smiling, obviously not wanting to undermine her professional assessment.

Saturday 16th April

Are electric shocks to the penis a good or bad thing? Our new quilt protector covers are great in terms of providing an additional lining and barrier that is easily washable. However, if the bedding is stripped off too quickly it rubs against the new protector covers and generates a lot of static electricity. In the last few weeks this has proved to be painfully problematic because I have received a number of jolting electric shocks after touching the metal frames of the beds whilst changing them. This is especially distressing when wearing some light linen shorts (there has been a mini heat wave of late) and your 'friend' down below brushes against the metal frame. For those who've never had an electric shock to the end of the penis, take my word, it's a rather unusual sensation – especially if you're not expecting it. Anyway, after a few such unsettling experiences, hopefully it will not happen again too frequently. If it does, of course, people may start thinking the shocks were being generated deliberately.

Sunday 17th April

All flights from UK airports were completely cancelled today following intelligence about a major security scare involving a terrorist plot to blow up planes using explosives in hand luggage. This evening a couple in their twenties checked in from Gatwick after being caught up in the ensuing chaos - Brighton only twenty-five miles from the airport.

'We're refugees from Gatwick,' they announced on arrival. 'It's been a nightmare. People stuck everywhere and no one with a clue what is happening, including the staff.'

'Where were you trying to get to?'

'Supposed to be flying to Ireland for my cousin's wedding tomorrow. Can't see us getting there now. Just hope things will calm down and try to get another flight early tomorrow morning. Looks like we're going to miss the wedding the way things are, which is a disaster. We've been looking forward to this for months. There will be tons of relatives and friends we haven't seen for years there - although a lot of them will be stranded as well.'

'No one wants to be blown up obviously but it seems a massive response to undertake. We had a group of Belgian guests who left this morning to catch a flight home which was also cancelled. Not sure what happened to them.'

'We couldn't believe it when we heard the news on the way to the airport. Even if some more sinister plans have been prevented, a lot of grief has still been caused to a lot of people. Shows how edgy things have become I guess.'

Monday 18th April

A middle aged male Danish guest was looking inquisitively today at our AA four-star accommodation classification sign on the wall.

'Excuse me, Scott. What do the letters "AA" stand for in this award?'

'Alcoholics Anonymous.'

'Is that true?' was the earnest reply after a thoughtful pause.

'No, I was only joking. The name of the organisation is actually called the Automobile Association,' informing him the truth as he didn't understand my humour.

Tuesday 19th April

An English couple in their fifties, whilst reading the newspapers at breakfast this morning, exclaimed astonishment out loud at a job advert in the paper.

'Incredible. It's not surprising people complain about falling quality of academic standards with salaries at this level. I can't imagine if Stephen Hawking was at a university in America it would be the same,' the wife declared to her husband.

After breakfast, intrigued at their conversation, I found the item referred to. It was a job advert for an assistant to Professor Hawking in the Department of Applied Mathematics and Theoretical Physics at the University of Cambridge. As well as being responsible for 'maintaining and improving his speech synthesis and computer support equipment' you would also 'help him to prepare and deliver seminars and public lectures and assist with scientific papers.' The salary would be on the Research Assistant scale £20,235 to £22,774 per annum 'with the starting salary depending on experience.'

Incredible indeed! And it's not April Fools Day either. The same salary level as the average twenty-two year old graduate and you are expected to not only assist a pre-eminent scientist and best-selling author with his theoretical physics papers but also to be able 'to maintain and improve' his computer support equipment. Still, if you are a really experienced candidate, you can at least claim the extra two thousand pounds at the top of the salary scale.

Wednesday 20th April

Brighton seafront is particularly pleasant in the mornings. The city has a transformed ambience before most people are up and prior to the extra hoards of day tourists that arrive, not to mention the contrast with the night when the drinkers emerge. It's especially serene when the sun rises over the English Channel horizon with clear blue skies and virtually no one else on the beach aside from seagulls whilst the quiet city skyline forms the backdrop.

After being up in the morning I normally stop at alternating newsagents, depending on the walking route taken, to buy the papers for the day. One of the regular shops visited is run by a guy called Tony who, in a resigned sort of way, has a droll sense of humour despite his often angst ridden cynical outlook. Usually at the time I arrive he is stooped over his counter reading the *Daily Mail* which I've often told him is bad for his health as he relates the latest 'doom and gloom' story about the parlous state of the nation. This morning, however, he was instead flicking through the hefty 'Society' section of *The Guardian* which carries hundreds of public sector job adverts related largely to different aspects of social work. Although a surprise change from his preferred read during the slow early trade, it did not prevent the typical greeting.

'Look at all these jobs in here. What a waste of time and money. This is what our taxes go on - busybody wasters creaming off billions from the government which people like us have to pay for,' he welcomed me with.

Not wanting to once more be associated as a fellow *Poujadist* I offered him an alternative view.

'Full of the joys of life again then? You know you could look at things in a more positive light. How about these jobs being a mark of a civilised country - doing much needed and worthwhile work? Or even creating a bit of social stability, keeping lots of people in secure, reasonably well paid work rather than on the dole - helps keep the shoplifters down to a minimum you know, the less of us who are unemployed.'

'Bollocks,' was the succinct retort.

Tony could be right; perhaps employing people to provide social welfare services doesn't provide any benefit? And if less people worked in the public sector and we all paid lower taxes maybe the private sector would 'mop up' to create equally alternative secure and well paid jobs? But if you look at low tax America with its huge social underclass, high violent crime, and vast inequality and insecurity compared to high tax Sweden with its highly educated population, low crime, and well paid egalitarian society, it surely would make sense to pay a little bit extra tax?

Thursday 21st April

We have a couple in their thirties staying who also read *The Guardian* so you might expect them to be left-of-centre types. Whilst talking to them, though, after mentioning the conversation with Tony yesterday, the couple were surprisingly hostile to the public sector.

'I've always been in favour really of higher government spending but after having direct experience in my job working with various quangos, I have to say I'm a bit more sceptical. The lack of accountability and waste with government money is incredible. There seems to have developed a whole new self-serving and self-perpetuating class of bureaucrats creating well paid jobs for themselves and not really doing anything of real use in their work. It's made me quite cynical,' one of them said.

There you go then. Perhaps the traditional left-right spectrum on tax and spend politics does no longer hold true? Or maybe it's just a case, for those who still believe in higher spending, to argue for it to be done more effectively for worthwhile achievements not just for self-serv-

ing waste. Keynes analogy of paying people to dig point-
less holes only for them to be filled in again could be apt
if such a self-perpetuating class does exist that perform
largely useless tasks. If government spending is to be
used to create employment and social stability and security, it might as well be done for something more gainful
than the metaphorical equivalent of just digging and
refilling some holes.

Friday 22nd April

A couple checked-in with the name of Mr. and Mrs.
Jones, obviously self-conscious of the connotations of
going for a 'dirty' seaside weekend break under the false
pretence of being a married couple.

'We know it's a common name but it is our real one
honest,' they quickly informed me straight after intro-
ducing themselves.

'It's ok,' I reassured them, 'I'm sure you would have
been "Mr and Mrs Smith" if you weren't married? You
are married aren't you?'

Saturday 23rd April

If it is true that Americans are generally more demand-
ing customers then we have just had a couple stay that
were a prime example of the stereotype.

First, was the late phone call the night before arrival
to cancel the last (and second) night of their stay without
expecting to be charged any costs despite the very short
notice. We agreed to this if the room could be re-let.

Second, on arrival, it was naturally assumed that eight items of luggage would **all** be carried up to the room by us.

Third, the request for an ice bucket – 'filled with ice' - should be taken to the room with a couple of champagne glasses.

Fourth, the additional request shortly after was to ask for an iron and ironing board to be taken to the room.

Fifth, about half an hour later, the demand was for a pair of scissors and sellotape because they 'needed to wrap up a present.'

Sixth, about twenty minutes after.

'You got a tape measure we could borrow. We want to make sure our hand luggage is the right size for the airport tomorrow.'

At the seemingly now regular interface of twenty to thirty minutes our American friends came to find us once more since their arrival, only a short time previous but beginning to feel like a lifetime ago.

'Scott. Sorry to bother you again but I need to borrow a screwdriver to tighten up one of our suitcases. If you give us a two or three different ones that should make sure we get the right size - and they have to be Philips as well.'

A while later the screwdrivers were returned but, of course, also with a further request being made (the eighth.)

'Could you bring up some additional coat hangers to the room? We have a lot of luggage that needs hanging up.'

(Yes, I know you have a lot of luggage; I carried it all to your room by myself.)

And then, on the way out for the evening, the American couple could not resist knocking on our door for a tenth time.

'Could you recommend some decent restaurants and directions how to find them?'

At breakfast this morning things continued on as usual.

'We would like our eggs very well cooked. Could you make sure they are flipped over so the yolk is hardened up and not runny at all?'

'Could we have some mustard with our breakfast. Have you got both English and French. We found we really like both of those mustards since travelling?'

'Scott, could we have an extra pot of coffee please. And could you put an extra scoop in - we like it real strong.'

'We'll be leaving at precisely 11.15am this morning so could you arrange for a taxi to be outside about a minute before this time.'

Ok. Let's be fair. None of these requests in themselves are too onerous or unexpected when you run a B&B - indeed all of them should really be standard for decent accommodation provision in the twenty-first century. In English culture, however, for better or worse, you are considered an awkward 'pain in the backside' if you repeatedly ask for too much. And rightly so in my opinion. If every guest knocked on our private door ten times a night to ask for additional extras we would go mad and the job would be impossible. Surely you would get a little embarrassed yourself as well, say after the fourth or fifth time? Make do without for goodness sake - can't you see you're now being irritating.

Still, it should be acknowledged that the Americans on departure did thank us for 'a lovely stay' and told us that we had 'been very helpful.' Never left a tip though?

Sunday 24th April

We noticed yesterday that the key for room five, which was not let for the night, was missing from our reception desk. I checked the room later and everything was ok so I went to bed. About 3am I woke up and couldn't get back to sleep. My mind drifted back to the missing key and I decided to go up and check the room again. I strongly smelt cigarette smoke as soon as I got to the corridor and there was also loud music playing from the room. As the master key would not work because the latch was down from the inside I started to bang hard on the door and shout for it to be opened, but there was no answer. Eventually, after threatening to call the police, the door finally opened and there was a scruffy man in his mid-twenties looking drugged up and surrounded by a cloud of cigarette smoke.

'What the hell are you doing in my house? How did you get the key? And what do you think you're doing smoking and with this music? This is akin to "breaking and entering" and I'm calling the police. And you're going to be paying for this night by the way as well.'

Immediately, saying nothing, the man grabbed a bag from the bed and literally jumped out of the third floor window and onto a ledge diagonally across which allowed him access onto our neighbours raised patio terrace. Any slippage, or if the ledge had not been reached, would have led to him being splattered in our backyard 50ft below. Obviously, and especially with reflection in the calm afterwards, there is a good chance the man was homeless and somehow had sneaked our key just to have a decent place to sleep for the night, but sympathy can only extend so far surely? It's not ideal really to find drugged-up strangers in the middle of the night abusing one of your bedrooms - even if the house is full up with other strangers (that you do know about) probably doing the same!

Monday 25th April

A three day booking had been made previously on behalf of someone else, which I had presumed was for a relative of the person who telephoned the reservation. Yesterday, a slightly overweight, but otherwise seemingly healthy middle aged woman turned up for this booking (a double en suite room on the first floor) - in Brighton to visit her daughter who was unwell in hospital.

At breakfast this morning, the same woman announced that she would not be staying for the remaining two nights already booked.

'I'm going to have to check-out early today. I'm sorry for any inconvenience but the [one] flight of stairs is just too much for me. The room is very nice and the guest house lovely but I will be leaving. I'm going to move somewhere else where there is a ground floor room or a lift.'

'Well that's ok. And thanks for telling us. But you know at such short notice, if we cannot re-let the room, we will have to make a charge. Otherwise we will lose money.'

'Yes. That's fine. Social services will pay anything due. Just speak to the woman who made the booking and she will sort the money out, no problem,' the woman replied with a smile.

What would Tony (the Poujadist shopkeeper) make of taxpayer money being spent in such a fashion?

Expensive double hotel rooms in the first place being paid by social services and then cancellation costs because one flight of stairs are not quite to preference - costs which were paid without question incidentally. No doubt also there is plenty of waste too in large private sector bureaucracies - although is that only a problem really for the relevant shareholders involved?

Tuesday 26th April

The Portuguese accent is very strange. Despite understanding Spanish to a basic level, which has many similar words, I have found it almost impossible to comprehend anything that a group of Portuguese guests staying at the moment say in their native language. In fact, although it is a Latin language and the people look distinctively Mediterranean, the heavy accent they speak sounds more like Russian or an Eastern European language. Apparently the origins of Portuguese are derived from the colloquial speech of a few Roman soldiers stationed at a fort on the west coast of the Iberian Peninsula. These soldiers would surely have been proud to know their own verbal idiosyncrasies would become the basis for a whole national language two thousand years on.

Wednesday 27th April

A woman came to the door in the late afternoon that I didn't recognise as ever seeing before.

'Is this where I stayed last night?'

'I don't think so. We only have a few rooms let at the moment and I'm fairly sure I know everyone that's here.'

'Oh damn. This is a right nightmare. I've left my bags somewhere and I can't remember where I stayed. I didn't think it was your place to be honest because your dining room is on the left of the door not the right. Thought I'd give you a try anyway.'

'Sorry. Maybe you should try our neighbours. Their dining room is on the right. And then perhaps every *other* B&B along the street?'

Thursday 28th April

'It's ever so kind of you to look after our bags. Please, have these chocolates as a thank you,' a mum and daughter said today, giving us an expensive box of truffles.

After about another fifteen 'thank you's and us also replying equally fifteen times that 'it was no inconvenience for us, honest,' we eventually said a final goodbye. This is exactly what you want - very friendly and polite guests who bring you chocolates, and also important, who can actually remember where they had stayed.

Friday 29th April

By contrast to yesterday the kind of guests you don't want are the ones that have a travel iron in the room and use the carpet as an ironing board. A burnt iron shape in the middle of the carpet is not the kind of 'boutique' design we were looking for in our rooms.

Saturday 30th April

A couple in their mid twenties came down to breakfast early this morning.

'We know it's ten minutes before the time but is it ok to have some breakfast now - I've got leave soon to make it to work in time?' the man politely asked.

'Yes, take a seat. Give us a minute and we'll be right with you.'

After serving them I was in the dining room again organising another table so started to make polite conversation.

'Had a nice break then and now back to the office?'

'Not exactly. I'm a professional paintballer and our team is in a tournament that starts this afternoon so I have to get off early to get there in time.'

'Oh really. That's interesting. I never knew professional paintballing existed. How long has that been around?'

'A while now but it's a lot bigger in the States - although it is growing over here. If we can get TV involved and then some bigger sponsorship for the league it should really take off. We're hoping to get someone like Richard Branson interested, especially now Virgin have their own TV channel.'

Beats the regular nine to five office job, instead get paid for mock war games. Perhaps the UK paintballers would have got a TV deal by the time you're reading this and it will be primetime viewing – inspiring a new generation of 'TA Time Bomb' types with a different career option.

MAY

Hemmeroid-injected meat?

Sunday 1st May

Accountancy. Accountancy. Where art thou, accountancy? It's another perk of being self-employed that you have the joys of maintaining your own accounts which, as commonly assumed correctly, is a rather mind-numbing and tedious procedure. Spending hour upon hour trailing through past receipts and totting up all other bills and expenditure can surely never be described as fun?

Perhaps, though, there is a deeper seated psychological basis for my accounts phobia. I remember my mum telling me when I was quite young, probably about junior school age, some early careers advice which came to haunt my psyche somewhat later. In retrospect it was most likely just some well-meaning encouragement, an aspirational parent trying to project some professional ambitions into her child, but the words have stayed embedded with me since.

'Well, Scott, you are very good with numbers. Accountants have to be good at maths and they earn a lot of money. You know you could do a lot worse than be an accountant when you are older.'

To be fair to myself I think my main ambition at the time was to be a professional footballer, a more than worthy goal (excuse the pun) when you are ten years old. The planted suggestion of my mum, however, along with the ego massage naturally of being told I was 'good' at maths was to supplant temporarily my dreams of football glory. These transposed hopes, however, were soon brought sharply into the real life focus of playground politics following a careers lesson a short time later. When all the other kids were still hoping to be footballers, astronauts, ballerinas, mermaids etc and you announce that you 'want to be a chartered accountant' you are obviously asking for trouble. I was to find this out the hard way and was rightly ridiculed for the staleness of my young (or should that be middle aged?) aspiration.

Since the emotional humiliation of this experience I probably have had an inner phobia which has resulted in a complete prejudice against all things related to accountancy. Perhaps this has skewed my psyche so far now that any potential enjoyment from filing through receipts and working out profit margins is completely unfeasible - or is it just repressed and secretly it gives me a thrill?

Monday 2nd May

Beware if travelling to the States! Be careful what you eat!

A newly-arrived American student, staying whilst waiting for his halls of residence to become available, was making conversation earlier today and made either a genuine speech mistake or maybe some deeper Freudian slip.

'Do you know of any good gyms around locally? I've put all this weight on after a motorbike accident last year. Really want to get back into shape now. It should be a lot easier to lose weight over here though because in the States there are too many hemmeroids injected into the beef. Hemmeroids are banned in Europe, right?'

'Do you mean hormone-injected meat not *hemmeroid*?' I asked to his acute embarrassment.

Maybe I should reassure him at breakfast tomorrow that all of our meat is definitely European and comes with a full guarantee of being completely 'hemmeroid free.'

Tuesday 3rd May

Does it matter if the English language evolves into a different form due to the large number of non-native speakers worldwide and because of the dominance of North American English?

To an English family staying at the moment – middle aged parents with two children in their late teens - it obviously does matter. At breakfast this morning the children were playing a word game out loud that basically consisted of uttering different 'American' phrases, which would not be used by English people, in a mocking transatlantic accent.

'Which team has the *winningest* record?'

'Please take all your belongings with you when *deplaning* the aircraft.'

'You need to *incentivise* yourself if you are going to do well.'

'The house was *burglarised*.'

Maybe such language, particularly the habit of turning nouns into verbs, is not a universal American phenomenon and could be equally mocked by many Americans themselves? Surely, though, the main thing that counts is whether you can understand and communicate with each other? After all, there are certainly plenty of regional skews of English in the UK itself which could be mocked, but would our language be as vibrant and colourful if they did not exist? Mind you, *winningnest*? No, some things are just wrong - the pedants are right.

Wednesday 4th May

Is it also wrong to use stereotypes? The children of the English family staying continued their language games again at breakfast this morning, only this time the emphasis was more on phrases that were 'stereotypical' North American - although once more were nearly all made in a derisive fashion (at least Americans can be flattered by their cultural significance even if it is negative.)

'Like, yeah, whatever dude' - *Beavis and Butthead* style.

'Don't talk to the face. Talk to the hand' - *Jerry Springer* guest style

'I want my burger and fries supersized' - ordinary *fat American* style.

And so on .... Imagine if such cultural scoffing was in reverse though? Would we be happy if foreigners thought we were all like guests on the *Jeremy Kyle* show? Or *Costa del Brit* types that always drink too much alcohol and only eat full English fry ups when abroad - 'none of that foreign muck.' Or all football hooligans?

It must be true that stereotypes are based somewhat on ignorance or a lack of familiarity which results in lumping together unknown individuals into a common misconstrued pot. Americans, of course, do typecast us back. I mean the ridiculous notion that English people have crooked and yellow teeth compared to American shiny white pearls all perfectly linear - clearly not true, is it?

Thursday 5th May

A regular part of running a B&B is the need to go to the supermarket on a near daily basis to get fresh supplies for breakfast. Most of the time it is quite enjoyable - getting out of the house, seeing the outside world and familiar faces - almost a key part of the social life that keeps the mental well being in check. Other times, however, going shopping 'for the business' can feel like a monotonous chore which is a forced errand and a waste of time. Today, was the latter mood, partly because I was in a hurry to get all work completed before a planned trip to the cinema. And this haste was not helped either by the tedious rant of the man in front of me at the check-out as he remonstrated over the price of his one tin of 'ultra-value' no-frills brand of hotdogs.

'These hotdogs are not twenty-six pence. You advertise these on the shelf as a special offer of only twenty-one pence. I will not pay the extra money.'

'I'm sorry sir if there has been mistake. If you take the tin and the receipt to the customer service desk just there, you will be able to get a refund if the price was wrong.'

'No I will not go over there. I bought seven tins of these hot dogs last week and had exactly the same problem. I was overcharged then and I will not be overcharged again. I want this sorted out right here.'

'There is nothing I can do here once the transaction has gone through. You will have to sort it out at the customer service desk.'

'I am not moving from here until the price is put through the till properly. And I will be contacting trading standards if it is not done.'

After continued remonstration and the queue at standpoint my own patience finally snapped.

'Look. Here's the five pence. Take it and then we can all move on.'

'This has nothing to do with you. You know nothing about what is going on here so just keep your busybody nose out.'

'We all just want to get home. Take the five pence, please. I don't mind, honest,' I once more kindly offered but as he defiantly crossed his arms with the marked intention of standing his hot dog ground there was no choice but to repack my basket and move to another check-out.

Friday 6th May

It's astonishing how many people do not enjoy their holidays - and factors not related peculiarly to our B&B either! A middle aged Australian couple from Brisbane, visiting their daughter in London but also travelling the UK, are typical of many guests we have had.

'We've been on holiday for six weeks now and I'm bloody sick of it,' the man announced to me as soon as he arrived. 'Had enough completely. Can't wait to get on that plane tomorrow and get back home.'

'Obviously haven't enjoyed being away then?'

'No. Don't get offended mate. I'm sure this is lovely house to stay and most of the other places have been as well. It's just bloody travelling. Eating out all the time;

lugging the suitcases on and off coaches; having to find the next hotel and not sleeping in your own bed. I just want to be in my own house and get back to my garden.'

It makes you wonder why some people ever bother to go away in the first place. Perhaps the expectation that you should be enjoying yourself adds further pressure to the holiday experience and creates a negative downward spiral as things do not work out as hoped? Maybe, though, in this particular case it was just the fact that the couple were Australian - they do have a bad reputation after all for their 'whingeing.'

Saturday 7th May

Speaking of Australian culture we have another couple with us at the moment from Sydney. Today we got into a conversation about the late Steve Irwin, the formerly exuberant television wildlife presenter. Despite the mass scenes of national mourning witnessed when he was killed by a stingray attack, it seems that a large number of his fellow compatriots (judging from the sentiments of these Australian guests anyway) did not share in that grief.

'Oh yeah, couldn't have happened to a nicer bloke' (with a heavily sarcastic tone.)

'You weren't a big fan then?'

'An embarrassment to Australia and a lot of other people back home feel exactly the same way. He showed no respect to animals when he filmed. Naturalists should be like David Attenborough - have some deference towards wildlife and leave them alone as much as possible. Got what he deserved in the end. Spend your whole life deliberately provoking wild animals into a reaction to make some "exciting" TV, you're asking for trouble ... not all Australians are idiot larrikins.'

Crikey! You ask a sensitive question about the perceived emotional distress of the loss of a national hero and get a vitriolic tirade thrown back instead. Wasn't he quite entertaining and pro-active in conservation and raising nature awareness? Perhaps, though, he represented a "cultural cringe" for some Australians which prevented even minor goodwill being shown towards his achievements?

Sunday 8th May

Normally we have at least a few couples in a week who immediately exclaim 'we are here to *escape* the kids for a few days' when asked about their reason for staying in Brighton (the other common reply being 'we are here to *escape* London.')

It is also frequent to have enquiries about 'family' rooms and accommodation away with children, often resulting in disgruntlement when informed that only children aged nine years and above are allowed to stay. Today, however, we had an enquiry on the phone about children with a slightly reversed emphasis.

'Is it still correct that you do *not* accept children?'

'Yes, not if they are aged under nine years old.'

'That's excellent. Both our immediate neighbours have young children and we want to escape their noise - it's driving us crazy. Are you absolutely sure though that there will be *no* children? We have been to other B&Bs before that have advertised "no children"

SCOTT BARFIELD

but there still always seem to be some there when we turn up.'

'I can promise you we do not have any children stay under nine years old. A large number of our guests are actually parents who are having a child-free break who appreciate the adult environment.'

'Superb. The only way I like children is barbecued and served with a large portion of chips. If there are definitely none in your house we would like to book a room please.'

Monday 9th May

Although sometimes I cannot resist joining in the conversations of guests in the dining room, more often it is a case of overhearing people talk which then stimulates the brain in all sorts of directions. A group of four this morning were discussing green issues and the conundrum of how rapid economic growth, particularly in China and India, is lifting millions out of poverty but also increasing environmental degradation.

Interesting stuff but a potential minefield of a topic to discuss, especially with guests. Can the West now preach to developing countries about pollution control when the vast majority of emissions still come from already advanced industrialised countries? Or why should land and forests in developing countries now be saved when we cut down most of ours hundreds of years ago? Save the rainforest and the tiger but not many in Europe are too keen to give back land to wilderness and live alongside re-introduced wolves and bears?

Anyhow, perhaps all these problems will be solved within a short space of time? At present the world economy is growing by an average of 5% a year which means wealth doubles approximately every fifteen years. Given the world economy is estimated at around $65 trillion and world population is roughly 6.5 billion then the average wage worldwide at the moment is about $10,000. Not brilliant but in fifteen years time, on the existing growth path, it will be $20,000, thirty years time $40,000, forty-five years time $80,000 and in sixty years the average person worldwide will be pulling in $160,000 a year - all in the equivalent of today's money. Hurrah, lets pop the champagne corks now for our grandchildren, all are going to be stinking rich - the lucky bastards.

Hold on, though. The more cynical might argue that even if wealth was in such abundance it would probably be so unevenly spread that poverty would still exist - one-third of the world millionaires with their yachts and private jets but a billion still in the slums. And what about the environment? Optimists point out that as people become richer they can afford to spend more on 'green' products. But there will be 10 billion people in sixty years time and on an average of $160,000 the world economy will have grown from $65 trillion now to $1600 trillion - can the planet cope with that?

Tuesday 10th May

The heavy ponderings of yesterday led to a few glasses of red wine being designated as a self-appointed reward – any old excuse. As often happens, one or two glasses more than necessary were drunk, and today is the hang-over. That's the problem with alcohol (and drugs) - they can be very 'moreish.'

Wednesday 11th May

The news and debate on the radio in the dining room is still dominated often by the complete mess in Iraq, which is not the most uplifting atmosphere for breakfast - thousands killed; the country's infrastructure and national heritage decimated; women being forced to wear the veil again; minority Christian and Jewish communities killed and forced out; female athletes, hairdressers, anyone selling alcohol and so on being murdered for their 'anti-Islamic' practices. Is this really better than Saddam?

Al Qaeda never existed before in Iraq whereas now they thrive, and what happened to those weapons of mass destruction? Imagine if Downing Street and all other government departments in Whitehall had been obliterated by bombs; along with prisons emptied of all prisoners; and the sacking of the whole army, police force and civil service; and also virtually no electricity and water supply?

Western intelligence must be an oxymoron surely. Of all the unpalatable countries to invade we chose Iraq – which had a secular government with a Christian deputy prime minister; promoted female literacy and education; and had abolished Sharia law courts.

Could two trillion dollars not have been better spent? Three thousand 'Millennium Domes' could have been built for the same money - fifteen each for every country in the world.

Thursday 12th May

Maybe some of the more disturbing Americanisms are actually starting to infiltrate our language. Today a marketing letter arrived in the post from agents, in the UK, looking for new clients seeking to sell their businesses.

'Because we have a lower tie-in contract period to sell your property we are more **incentivised** to find a buyer.'

Too many people have obviously been attending 'Motivate Yourself to be a Millionaire' type seminars. Could it be counter-productive though when trying to make money to sound too much like an American business school manual?

Friday 13th May

Sometimes, when receiving emails, there can be something about the way questions are phrased that makes you wary about the type of person making the enquiry. A few weeks ago we had a couple of such emails from a man who sounded extremely pernickety and a right potential 'Mr Bean' nerdy pain.

'I have found your website on the internet but would like to clarify a few points first before deciding whether to book. Please find these points listed below:

(1) As I am a tall man - 6ft 7inches in fact. Please could you clarify whether your showers would be appropriate for a man of my height? There has to be ample space for me to stand up and for the shower head to be adjusted sufficiently above my head. Please

inform me of the height of your showers / shower-head adjustment?

(2) Because of my height I would require an extra top sheet to be provided that needs at least an extra two feet length (over the bed size) so that it can tucked into all four corners of the bed. This will allow my feet to be kept warm because they normally stick out the end of the bed.

(3) Please could you confirm the parking arrangements of your establishment?

(4) Would soya milk be available for breakfast because I am allergic to dairy milk?

(5) Are there any discounts for single occupancy of a double room?'

Having sent a brief reply, which included reference to our superking size beds that diagonally would easily accommodate a man of 6ft 7inches; we were sort of hoping the man would not reply. However, he did eventually book online (after further email questions) and turned up yesterday with instant drama on arrival.

'Oh hello. Please, please will you help me. I'm so stressed. I've been driving around for thirty minutes now without finding a parking space. I'm so so stressed. Please help me. This is awful. I'm just so stressed. I just want you to come and get in the car with me and help me find somewhere. My car is just parked there on double yellow lines for now. Would you please come with me and help me park, please,' was the near hysterical greeting as I met the *tall guy* for the first time.

'Hello. Glad you've arrived and don't panic. If there are no spaces on this street you should be ok on the next street down. And, if there are still no spaces there, you can park in the NCP three streets the other way - about a minute walk from here,' I said trying to calm his rather frayed nerves.

'Oh could you not come and sit in the car with me. I'm terrible at parallel parking as well even if there is a space. Please could you come with me?' he again pleaded.

'I'm sorry but I need to be here in the house for other arrivals. It really should not be too much of a problem to park. You're welcome to unload your bags whilst the car is here but I can't come with you,' I replied once more with a growing sense that my first instincts about this booking were going to prove more than correct.

About fifteen minutes later the *tall guy* returned having found a space for his car. Although initially he seemed much calmer than previous it did not take him too long before he started to get flustered again.

'Now about the bed,' he asked almost immediately after stepping into the house. 'As you can see I am 6ft 7inches tall so will have a problem with my feet sticking out the end of the bed. Do you have a top sheet available for me that can be tucked in over all four corners?'

'Well, as I explained in the email, we don't have a top sheet but the bed is superking size which measures about nine feet on the diagonal. And we do also provide bedspreads. I'm sure the bed will be big enough for you.'

'Ok. Ok. Alright then. I had a feeling you would be funny about this so I brought my own anyway,' he replied whilst pulling a top sheet out of his bag to defiantly show me.

6ft 7inches tall. 6ft 7inches tall. How many times do you want to inform me of your height? You're hardly suffering from gigantism. Stop thinking you're so bloody exceptional. In fact why not just stuff a 'top sheet' in it.

Saturday 14th May

All four corners meticulously tucked in and perfectly straight.

Sunday 15th May

Revelling in the perils of their wildlife is another national sport for Australians according to a couple staying with us from Sydney. And adding as much extra bravado as possible to the wildlife hazards particularly applies apparently when dealing with new *Pommie* immigrants/tourists.

Although, of course, now sceptical that all conversation about Australia was embellished it was interesting to hear that shark meat used to be the norm when ordering fish and chips up until the last few years. Overfishing though has now drastically reduced numbers which has also made it a lot less common to encounter sharks whilst swimming in the Sydney area ('the waters were absolutely teeming with sharks when we were young.') Funnel web spiders as well are supposed to be a lot rarer these days because new houses are brick-built with inside toilets and much greater spraying of insecticides – 'all the same we still have great fun at the expense of you *Poms*. We always tell you the place will be crawling with spiders everywhere.'

Monday 16th May

Julie Burchill, the Brighton-based journalist and writer, has often commented that the 'white indigenous English working class are now the one group you can insult without feeling the breath of the Commission for Racial Equality on your neck' and how the recent phenomenon of denigrating 'chavs' is equated to what she terms 'social racism.' Although, undoubtedly she would consider me to be one of the 'jokers' who always reassure her that not **all** the working classes are wasters, surely distinguishing chavs out as a separate group is fair enough?

Even before the term was invented it was the chav minority in my school days that used to make life a misery for everyone else - bullying, constant classroom riots, abuse of the 'paki' kids etc. Why should there *not* be a differentiated labelling of such a group from the ordinary working class?

And now, in running a B&B, the need for a distinction continues. Ordinary working class guests behave no different from the middle classes - always a few rare exceptions in both groups but mostly no problem. Chavs, though, by definition almost, are not the same. When you find bits of kebab left all up the stairs carpet the night before, or the doorbell goes at 4am in the morning to a spitting burger-munching idiot who has lost his key, or a couple stay in bed hours after check-out despite frequent requests to vacate the room for new arrivals, or a room is left like a pigsty with lager stains sprayed up the wall - you know when these things occur that it will be the chav guests causing the problem.

Now, of course, it is not the aim to be some deluded snob desperate to cement a further unnecessary class division in the nation. It is understood that if Bill Sikes has been your dad for the past eight generations since peasant ancestors were kicked from the countryside into urban slums, then you will not have been dealt the best start in life. But, still, knowing such facts does not help if you are in a school where the teachers spend half their time dodging chalk and chairs being thrown at them. And it does not help too much either when inviting strangers into your house running a B&B and expecting some basic behavioural norms.

Perhaps Julie Burchill is right to be so charitable and understanding to the plight of the undeserving 'bad proles' whilst highlighting the pretentious superiority of the more deserving 'good proles?' Other countries after all that were not so vigorous in transforming peasants into industrial factory fodder do not seem to have the same 'chav' problem we do. It is interesting though that despite boasting of 'falling down drunk with vomit' with her fellow chav comrades, Julie Burchill usually prefers drinking in such establishments as the *Groucho Club* not the *Hawk and the Dove* on my old council estate – does that mean she would not really welcome our next chav guests being sent round to her house instead for the night?

Tuesday 17th May

This morning the *tall guy* kindly left a number of separate post-it notes on the shower door instructing us to 'Change the towels' - 'Empty bin' – 'Clean Shower' – 'Clean sink' - 'Do **not** re-make the bed.'

Wednesday 18th May

We have two young men from Thailand staying with us for a week, a fact that I didn't initially connect with the 'Thai Lady Boy Dance Show' that visits Brighton every year. Closing up this evening, two young women came into the doorway, sexily dressed and with lots of make up.

'Could I help you,' I asked, not recognizing either woman.

'Scott. It is us. Aroon and Kiet from room five.'

'Pardon,' I responded as my brain struggled again to recognise the women.

'It is us. Aroon and Kiet from room five. We are appearing in the show in town and have just come back to get something from our room. Can we come in?'

'Oh,' I exclaimed, as it suddenly dawned on me that they were both Lady Boy performers and in dress. 'I'm sorry. I never realised that's why you were in Brighton. Please come in.'

'Thank you,' they smiled at me with a respectful Thai bow of the head, 'You should come and see the show. It is very good. We will get you tickets.'

It should have been less surprising really, especially as I had been amused earlier by men being hoodwinked in the local supermarket by some other Asian 'women' in high heels wiggling their way, exhibition style.

Thursday 19th May

A team of cyclists are staying who are racing competitively in a five-day event in Sussex. One of the riders is quite a bit smaller than the others and was being teased at breakfast this morning by the rest of the team. Apparently the small rider had won the first stage race but made the mistake of telling his team mates what his Scottish mother had said when congratulating him on the phone.

'Oh, Alistair love. Haven't you done ever so well. And especially against all those other big strong men,' was the repeated mimic to much laughter.

Friday 20th May

The *tall guy* wedged pillows between the headboard and the mattress, thus making the (superking size) bed slightly longer by leaving an overhang of an extra few inches. This did not affect though all corners of the 'extra' long sheet from being tucked in appropriately.

Saturday 21st May

Two jolly Dutch couples at breakfast this morning were telling me how it is common for English people to mistake their accents for German.

'We don't like being called Germans though,' one of them added before immediately then launching into an impersonation of Basil Fawlty.

'Don't mention the war! Don't mention the war!'

As all four of them curled up with laughter, and me amused at Dutch people doing an impression of an English hotelier getting flustered about Germans, I remembered reading a story recently about how Dutch football fans always chant a joke when playing Germany about returning bicycles that en mass were confiscated from Holland in the war.

'Speaking of Germans. Have they given back your bicycles yet?'

No, apparently is the answer, but it took them a while to tell me as they rolled around belly laughing.

Sunday 22nd May

Overheard a middle aged English couple talking this morning about the Japanese with the man referring to them as 'a cruel race,' which is a sentiment I've heard many times before from older English people. Understandable, perhaps, that the war generation is prejudiced against the Japanese but it's interesting how the same 'cruel race' phrase always seems to be the specific description used. How did that originate and become so embedded?

Anyhow, following on as well yesterday from my capitulation to the Dutch in mocking the Germans, it is an irony that the best behaved and friendliest guests that stay with us are the Japanese and Germans. Is there any connection with this finding and the war? Are the Japanese and Germans still *apologising for the war* (as Harry Enfield's 'German' character would say) by being so over polite in reverse now? Or is there a link to both countries having an authoritarian past? Or maybe it's just because the two countries are so prosperous and well educated in the present day? Perhaps there could be a potential PhD thesis for someone - 'Cultural Benefits of an Authoritarian History and Losing a War.'

Monday 23rd May

The Today programme on the radio at breakfast this morning had a piece about the re-opening of the Gleneagles hotel in Torquay, which was the reported inspiration for *Fawlty Towers* following a stay there by the Monty Python team in the 1970s. Precisely on queue, just as I walked into the dining room carrying two plates, the radio started blasting out the theme tune for the hit comedy and everybody turned towards me smiling. The next time I entered the dining room the presenter was relaying the story of the 'shambolic hotel where the owner hates all his guests.'

Tuesday 24th May

Seeing eggs being cooked every morning it never ceases to amaze me that this food is actually the foetus potentially of an unborn animal. Strange food to eat when you think of it like that. Still, probably best to just leave the wording on our menus as 'eggs' rather than changing it to 'bacon, sausage and unborn animal foetus.'

Wednesday 25th May

More bad news on the radio this morning about fatalities of British soldiers in Iraq, the latest victims being blown up in roadside bombs. As *Texas Guinan* said, 'a politician is a fellow who will lay down your life for his country.' Even worse in this case though because *our* country never faced any threat in the first place.

Thursday 26th May

We have a right bunch of stony-faced, miserable gits in at the moment. Blimey! You are all on holiday, cheer up, it's depressing me. When you stay in this B&B it's a two-way hospitality experience so stop being so dour. Laugh and the world laughs with you etc. so at least try and meet me halfway. Perhaps this lot though are all a bit too uninspiring to find something to be enthused about? Brings Leonard Rositer to mind - 'If ignorance is bliss why aren't more people happy?'

Friday 27th May

We have two middle aged Danish women staying with us on a teaching exchange who are both a bit 'Ann Widdecombe' in dress and mannerism.

'Are all the pubs and restaurants around here gay?' one of them exclaimed to me today. 'We really did not know we would be staying in a red light district.'

'The area is very mixed and not a red light district at all - being gay is not the same as being a prostitute,' I told them.

Saturday 28th May

The London to Brighton event today was a rally for minis. Not as big as the VW rally, nor quite the same lifestyle type devotion, but nevertheless a product brand that still seems to evoke a particular type of enthusiastic brand loyalty.

Sunday 29th May

Concentrated orange juice is packed with more than enough of its own sweetness. The brand we serve at breakfast is fairly standard, not particularly different from other makes in its sugar levels. If you do not have a sweet tooth, however, the sticky film left encased in your mouth will make you run quickly to brush your teeth to prevent the feeling of instant decay setting in.

Spanish people, on the subject of tolerance to sugar, seem to live in a different stratosphere from 'normal' sweet-toothed mortals. We have become accustomed now to Spaniards using huge numbers of sugar sachets when drinking coffee and with cereals, but this morning we noticed a couple from Madrid taking extra sugar sachets from an empty adjacent table to pour into their glasses of orange juice. Wow! Topping up concentrated orange juice with additional teaspoons of sugar?

Spaniards are renowned incidentally for their salt intake as well. So much so, in fact, that an expression exists in Spain - 'sin sal' - which is used in a derogative fashion to describe people who have a dull personality (the literal translation of *sin sal* being *without salt*.)

Monday 30th May

A mixed race couple arrived today - a white man and an attractive Asian lady who looked very similar to a girl who used to be in my class at school. Seeing them happily together brought back some distinct and uncomfortable memories from the prevailing social climate that existed in the 1980s (at least in my particular suburb of west London and comprehensive school where 90% of the population was white) in which it was socially unacceptable to even contemplate dating a member of the opposite sex who was from a different ethnic background. I can clearly recall a general conversation amongst a large number of my male school peers in direct relation to the Asian girl in my class:

'Yeh, she's definitely one of the prettiest girls in the year but there's no way you can go out with a Paki, is there?' was a typical sentiment expressed.

Aside, of course, from the sad bigotry was the self-defeating waste of a potential opportunity - view someone as attractive only to deny any possibility of romance? And also to compound the ignorance, the attractive Asian girl in my class was actually from Bangladesh. Regardless whether someone was from Pakistan, India or Bangladesh - or whether Muslim, Hindu or Sikh - all were viewed by a large number under the same pejorative all-encompassing term 'Paki.' Surely today's generation has moved on from then?

Tuesday 31st May

Perhaps cultural awareness and tolerance does still have some way to go? Some Punjabi's, in response to the terrorist bombings in London, have been wearing t-shirts on the underground which read 'Don't Freak, I'm a Sikh!' Or maybe this is just an example of multicultural humour in a harmonious modern society? Mind you, given that a 'paediatrician' was recently hounded out of his home following a campaign by a local newspaper against convicted paedophiles, society may not be quite there yet.

JUNE

Wedding night threesome?

Wednesday 1st June

The news on the radio for weeks now has been unrelenting in blanket tedious coverage of the Labour Party leadership succession and the internal relationship dynamics of the personalities. Please! Change the tune a bit; it's ruining the atmosphere of the dining room. All the interesting news and events in the world and we have to listen to dreary (mostly male) journalists talking endlessly about the leadership contest. My theory for this overemphasis is that overly competitive Neanderthal males care more about boy's pissing games and who is the biggest monkey rather than what is actually important in the world.

Thursday 2nd June

We never learn do we? Older Brits are just as bad as students and young people. A social night out with the neighbours inevitably led to a few drinks too many and the exact details of any conversation being lost from the memory. This means next time we all see each other it will be a 'groundhog day' experience with no previous reference points to help any new conversation along - or maybe it will just be *me* sadly repeating myself?

One scary different thing though when you do drink to excess when older – seeing Keith Richards looking back in the mirror the next morning.

Friday 3rd June

'Sorry but Pride weekend is the busiest weekend of the year so you can't have a room just for the Saturday night. It is a three night minimum stay.'

'But I'm straight. I'm not coming for Pride weekend.'

'It's not a minimum stay *only* for gay people! You're still welcome to stay if you're straight but it has to be for three nights.'

'That's stupid.' Phone slammed down.

Saturday 4th June

Last night we had a couple of newlyweds arrive but unfortunately there were three of us in the room together for longer than ideal on a romantic wedding night. A few weeks previous the man had made the reservation from London but had not said anything about a 'honeymoon' stay. All he requested was a *superior twin room* on the first night and then a *standard double room* for the following two nights. Specific arrangements were also made for a late check-in but when they actually turned up it was approaching midnight, a considerable time later than arranged. Without prior warning or a good reason I would normally be slightly peeved at such a late hour. However, when they did finally arrive, the wedding gown and groom's suit indicated straight away that they were newlyweds. My quickly summoned congratulatory greeting, though, was rapidly overshadowed by the realisation that the twin room had been booked for their first night.

'You've booked the superior twin room for tonight. Was it actually two separate single beds you wanted or did you really want a double bed?' I asked, not wanting to be presumptuous, but clarifying that surely they had meant to book a double bed for their wedding night.

'Oh no,' the man replied as his new wife looked on anxiously. 'Is a twin room not a double bed? I thought that was the best type of room available. No we definitely want a double bed.'

Again, normally, at such a late hour I would not be so accommodating but as they were newlyweds I agreed to remake their room up - the twin beds were *zip n' link* and so could be converted to a superking size double. The only issue really was the uneasy atmosphere as I tried to make conversation for the fifteen minutes it takes to re-change the bed. The woman was distinctly unimpressed and frosty towards her new husband as she stood there in her wedding gown and romantic 'bridal suite' waiting for me to finish the room.

This morning as well the man came to down to breakfast by himself.

'The wife is still in bed but I didn't want to miss the full English,' he said.

I have upgraded their next two nights for free to the same superior room – hopefully that will help kick-start the matrimonial passion a bit better.

Sunday 5th June

A few weeks ago a journalist from the Sunday Times phoned up asking for the opinion of a small hotelier on the proposals for a new 'bed tax' on hotel accommodation to help fund local government. I duly responded with a few reasons why it would be a negative thing; bad for the struggling domestic tourist industry competing with sunnier foreign destinations; detrimental for the balance of payments with less overseas visitors; unfair penalising of the hotel industry etc (whilst omitting the real main reason, of course, that I would personally lose out financially). Anyway I decided to type in 'bed tax' to the Sunday Times website today and see if any article had actually ever been written. And what do you know; there I was, being quoted as a spokesperson for the hotel industry. Famous, finally! Could get addictive, having your name in print.

Monday 6th June

Fresh in my new role as spokesperson for the hotel industry I've been thinking more generally about politics. Trouble is, most domestic politics is actually fairly boring - endless arguments over a very narrow range of issues. Tweedledee Party will tax and spend this amount of national income whereas Tweedledum Party will tax and spend 1% less. Whoopee!

Instead, it's much more exciting to fantasise about a world where everything is sorted and politics is just an administration framework that facilitates 'real' life. We can all concentrate then on enjoying ourselves and living and creating culture - a bit utopian maybe?

Tuesday 7th June

Continuing the theme of utopia, or perhaps that should more accurately be dystopia, I read an article today which quoted Marilyn Manson arguing that he's glad

George Bush was elected because culture is more interesting and productive when society is troubled and divided. One way of putting a positive spin on things, but not sure the Republicans will be using the slogan: 'Vote for us - We'll mess things up so bad, culture will thrive.' Not convinced either that those in Iraq have 'at least' seen a cultural renaissance as compensation for all the strife and instability caused?

Wednesday 8th June

'We definitely will stay for two nights. We may also stay a third night but we don't want to commit at the moment.'

A day later.

'Do you know yet if the room will be needed for the third night? We may have someone else wanting to book it but obviously you have first refusal.'

'Sorry if we're messing you around but we're still not sure. Don't hold it back for us though. We'll just have to find alternative arrangements if need be. Our son was killed in a car crash last year and we're here for the inquest into his death. We just don't know exactly how long it will all last for.'

'Really sorry to hear that. Don't worry about the room either. We'll keep it open for you regardless.'

How important is maximising room revenue?

Thursday 9th June

A team of four male electrical engineer contractors turned up looking for two twin rooms for the night. Apparently the four of them had spent a long time searching around and were tired of knocking on doors without much success. When informed that we only have one twin room and one double room left remaining the two younger guys in the team dismissively shook their heads.

'Look, it doesn't matter. We don't mind sharing the double for the night. We just need to find somewhere to stay and your place looks nice.'

'Yeah, we're not homophobic like the boss [nodding towards the older man in his late fifties]. He'd be a bit funny about sharing a bed so you'd better give him the twin. We'll be happy with the double. Just somewhere to crash for the night. No problem.'

As the younger men seemingly had an easygoing nature I made a light-hearted joke when showing them up to their double room.

'Ok guys. Here is your room. Just be careful of any of those *Brokeback Mountain* [the "gay cowboy" film] feelings when in bed.'

When this quip was greeted with a distinctly frosty silence I handed the key with a wry smile and quickly left them all alone (to their double bed.)

Friday 10th June

Aaargh. Bloody hangovers. I feel the need to unscrew the top of my head. Take my brain out. Give it a bloody good scrub and clean. And put it back in completely toxin free.

Saturday 11th June

How self-aware are the upper middle classes about their privileged lifestyles and how perceived by others? A group of four posh women in their early forties are having a 'college reunion' and every morning in the dining room talk so loudly that everyone else clearly overhears them. Is the self-satisfied conversation aimed more at impressing their friends or the surrounding strangers passively eavesdropping?

'Oh Arabella's progressing fantastically well with her piano lessons.'

'It can be a beastly awful journey to the tennis club at times.'

'The towels at my new gym are just divine and the new soap dispensers are absolutely fabulous.'

'When we were in Kenya ....'

'Well when we went to South Africa ....'

'Yes. That's exactly what we found with our French cottage.'

'I'm terribly impressed with how quickly Toby is picking up French.'

'The pony club is marvelous ...'

'.....'

Sunday 12th June

A couple arrived yesterday for a few days away for the woman's thirtieth birthday.

'Not really something to celebrate though, is it?' the women stated with a genuinely glum expression.

'You're still young, *honest*,' I replied, trying to lift the mood at the start of their holiday. 'Thirty is a good mile-stone. Pop the corks tonight to usher in an exciting new decade.'

'Hmm. Maybe.'

At breakfast this morning the woman was again look-ing far from cheerful. And when her partner ordered white toast with his breakfast she solemnly followed with, 'Well I guess I should have brown toast really and be healthy.'

'Don't tell me,' I said to her. 'Up until yesterday you would have always ordered white. Maybe your thirties aren't so good, hey?'

'Definitely not.'

Monday 13th June

Is there a certain age when the great jollity from getting drunk is not worth the hangover the next day - if such a utilitarian trade-off is possible? Perhaps in the same way that most people who experiment with drugs when younger give them up because the inevitable downer eventually far outweighs the high? Or maybe drugs of some sort for all ages will always be in demand, just that middle aged people only need something to get them through the evening's television not to go dancing until 6am in the morning?

Tuesday 14th June

A man knocked on the door today to read the gas and electricity meters. He quickly flashed an identity card at me, not giving me enough time to see it properly, but I duly showed him in to the meters anyway as he was wearing a jacket that had a small 'Seeboard' logo. No problems. Then, however, about two minutes after the 'meter inspector' had left, I suddenly realised that both our gas and electricity accounts were with British Gas not Seeboard. Now perhaps meter reading is not necessarily undertaken by the company that holds your account, or maybe this particular inspector had just got his addresses mixed up? Either way, it makes you realise how easy it is to gain access to someone's house by simply flashing a card and asking to come in. Next time a stranger knocks on my door to 'read the meter' I'll keep a closer eye on the side table where my wallet normally resides.

Wednesday 15th June

Walking up the stairs today, the corridor stunk of cannabis. Inside one of the rooms it smelt even worse and there were stripped down cigarette butts and tobacco all over the bed.

'You know it's strictly non-smoking throughout the whole house as it clearly states on these signs,' I later said to a young couple when they returned.

'We haven't smoked any cigarettes.'

'Non-smoking obviously includes the burning of the cannabis resin and smoking of the joints.'

'The joints were smoked out of the window. And we definitely wouldn't smoke cigarettes inside the room.'

Thursday 16th June

What percentage of people actually get on well with their neighbours? Or, perhaps more interestingly, how many people end up having some kind of dispute? Up until today, relations have always been reasonably cordial (with our non-bondage neighbours) - leaving aside, of course, the irritating noise we often hear from regular vodka fuelled parties, always accompanied with *Queen* and *Meatloaf* karaoke singing, and usually followed by a blazing domestic row shortly afterwards. Anyway, today, all pretence of friendly relations were dramatically blown away when our (highly strung) neighbours decided to vent some of their neurosis and obvious marriage and general life disharmony towards us, rather than against each other.

'I need to have a word with you. We've got problems in our house and it's all coming from your side. And we're not happy about it. There's damp in our walls and nails sticking out all over the place. It's been caused by your building work and we want something done about it,' was the aggressively spoken greeting.

'Are you talking about the same issue you raised six weeks ago? I thought this had all been resolved - the problem has nothing to do us.'

'Nothing has been resolved but it *is* going to be sorted now,' was the continued menacing tone, somewhat lacking in any sense of diplomacy.

'Look, if it is the same issue, there is no further way forward other than to get an independent surveyor in to assess the situation. Like I said before, we would then pay if the source of the problem was found to be from our building. But as our builders identified last time - the damp is most likely coming from the old tiles on your roof that have been patched up before and now need re-doing again or replacing.'

'Oh yeh. That's right. It would be our fucking roof. Not the fault of your monkey fucking builders.'

'It's not just my builders. I've had a second opinion from different builders and I've also spoken separately to surveyors at the local council. Everyone has said the same - the problem is almost certainly something internal to your house, especially as there is no sign of any damp on our side.'

'Yeh. Fucking load of rubbish. I suppose all the nails through my wall are the fault of my roof as well, yeh?'

'We covered this before as well. The work we had done was only in the front rooms of our house. We would have had to use zigzag nails that were 3ft by 12ft by 3ft to go through to where you are saying. It's impossible to be from our house.'

At this point the neighbour's wife, who had obviously been listening, came out onto their steps and started hollering across at me in a voice so loud the whole street could hear.

'Please Scott. Will you just sort this out for us,' she wailed. 'You don't understand. I'm on anti-depressants. I can't take anymore of this. We just want to sell up and move. I can't sleep at night. Please do something.'

Although completely taken aback now by the aggression of the male neighbour, followed by the unexpected public hysteria of his wife, there was still nothing more I could offer to remedy the situation.

'Look, I'm sympathetic to any problem you have, but you can't just assume that it's my fault. The only way to fix this problem is to find out the real cause behind it.'

'I'm on anti-depressants,' the wife again shrieked over to me. 'Do you not understand?'

After another twenty minutes of the same sort of highly charged conversation being played out in the street, only going around in the same circle, all three of us eventually called it a day with no resolution. I can't wait to bump into them again sometime shortly.

Friday 17th June

So many people start conversations with us in relation to 'what it is actually like to run a B&B?' Obviously it's a business that people are interested in, probably reflected in the proliferation of TV programmes which cater to those seeking (or being voyeuristic towards) such a lifestyle. Such inquisitiveness is generally fine; it can be flattering when strangers are so curious about the life you have chosen to lead. However, frequently, there are questions asked which have a direct tone of pity for an *assumed* life of hard work and exhaustion. Although the somewhat patronising tone of this kind of sentiment is normally well-meaning and implicitly sympathetic, quite often the motives seem a little more ostensible. A couple today were a good example of how, perhaps, commiseration could really just be a cover for belittlement.

'It must be ever such hard work running a B&B. Do you *ever* get any time off?'

'And having to wait in all the time for people to arrive - I guess it really ties you to staying in the house?'

'How do you *cope* with getting up to serve breakfast? That must be really difficult to do *every* morning?'

'I imagine you've had some problem guests stay as well. Have you ever had to call the police?'

'It just seems like so much work for two people. I don't think we could do it.'

When faced by such persistent and unrelenting - *just exactly how shit is your life?* - lines of questioning, the obvious knee-jerk response is to refute every negative assumption with a positive antidote.

'Well, it's great being your own boss …'

'It's much better than a nine-to-five office job. I wouldn't fancy that …'

'Not much of a commute when you work here - just step out of your bedroom door …'

'Doesn't have to be hard work. Depends on how much money you want to earn. Work two days a year or three hundred and sixty-five. You can choose exactly your work/life balance …'

Ok. Ok. Maybe I'm being a bit over-sensitive. Perhaps I'm just narked really because there is an element of truth in every negative assertion made. Rather than get wound up, however, I should perhaps just realise that most people are not really being disparaging, just frustrated with themselves – some perverse comfort in hoping others are also miserable and stressed?

Saturday 18th June

'Where can we find all the nightlife then darling,' asked two overweight middle aged sisters, wearing clothes far too small for them, when they arrived yesterday – potential trouble foreboding.

'We don't like to complain,' said a nice American couple at breakfast this morning, 'but there was an awful lot of shouting and noise last night from the room next door to us and we could also smell cigarette smoke strongly.'

Then, right on queue, the endearing Fat Sisters waddled into the dining room.

'Sorry darling. We've only gone and locked ourselves out of our room. Alright if we just have breakfast first before you let us back in.'

Not wanting to cause a scene in front of all the other guests I took the breakfast order and then immediately went upstairs to check the state of things. The corridor absolutely reeked of cigarette smoke and a full length mirror from the hallway was missing from the wall. Inside the Fat Sisters' room, aside from the stench of cigarettes and general mess, was the hallway mirror propped haphazardly with a large crack in it. The drinking glasses we supply were also filled with numerous cigarette butts floating in murky black water.

Although wanting to explode at them as soon as going back downstairs I waited until breakfast was over and there were no other guests around.

'We've had other guests complain about loud noise from your room last night and also about cigarette smoke. The whole place up there stinks of cigarettes. And what do you think our drinking glasses are for? Do you really think our next guests want to drink out of a glass that has had putrid tar water stagnating in it for hours? And what about the mirror?'

'We only put the butts in the glasses because we didn't have an ashtray - better than putting them in the bin. And the mirror was definitely already cracked before we took it.'

'I think it's just best you leave immediately please,' I said, not being bothered to remonstrate any further.

Sunday 19th June

It was the turn of more cyclists for the London to Brighton rally of this weekend. Twenty-eight thousand participants for the fifty mile journey equal an awful lot of bicycles arriving in town. Most, including half our guests, were staying in town for the night after the strenuous trip. Predictably the cycle stands were soon completely full and there wasn't too much railing space left by the evening either.

Monday 20th June

Two French couples staying the last week have stereotypically (which has also proved to be the norm generally with French guests) eaten only croissants every day for breakfast - not swayed once to taste the 'Full English' choice on the menu. Perhaps that is the secret of the French paradox? You are able to smoke cigarettes and eat high fat foods without getting a dodgy ticker as long as you never 'binge eat.' Or maybe it's the red wine, garlic, and two month long summer holidays?

Tuesday 21st June

At midnight last night the bell repeatedly and persistently started ringing. As I went up to answer the door (after getting out of bed and dressed) the young, posh 'Rugger Bugger' type that had been staying in the first floor room at the front of the house came running down the stairs.

'Oh you must be joking. I've just had to bloody climb up onto the balcony to get in through the window. Don't tell me you've been in all this time. Did you not hear the bell?'

This was particularly annoying on a number of counts and provoked a rant which was, perhaps, a little too aggressively spoken.

'Excuse me. Do you not think *you* should be apologising instead for disturbing me and other guests that have been woken by the doorbell being constantly pressed? It is *your* fault, not mine that *your* key was left in the room and it's taken you until midnight to sort it out. And why not just wait a few minutes before choosing to break into the house? I'm not the one who "must be joking" - you "bloody" are.'

The two of them did not come down to breakfast this morning.

Wednesday 22nd June

Just as some toast was about to be served at breakfast today I noticed, with horror, green-blue mould on one of the corners. Now, honestly, we are an establishment which takes pride in being clean and hygienic. The bread was only opened the previous day and not past the sell-by date, so should have been ok. It serves warning though - keep a close eye on food quality regardless of what the supplier advises. Thankfully no other guests had already been served any toast unnoticed from the same batch - guessing most people would probably prefer jams and marmalade on their toast to mould?

Thursday 23rd June

Coincidentally, or perhaps not, we went out for a meal yesterday evening and encountered a similar hygiene problem to our experience earlier in the day. The plates the waitress laid down in front of us, much to her embarrassment, were still 'cemented' in old food stains. I'm sure, however, that many other restaurants have encountered the same problem when unloading dishwashers without checking properly as plates are quickly piled up. Our ingenious solution, although slightly ridiculous, is to wash all the plates (and cutlery) before actually putting them in the dishwasher.

Friday 24th June

In with the zeitgeist of being eco-friendly and, of course, completely self-focused also in perhaps boosting business with a 'green' image, we have been researching the feasibility of putting solar panels and a wind turbine on our roof. Today, however, it has just been announced that the £3.5 million fund allocated by the government for subsidy grants for renewable technology installation has already been used up. Amazing! In the same week the prime minister warns gravely of only a 'ten to fifteen year window of opportunity to prevent *catastrophic* climate change' the paltry £3.5 million help for households to create carbon-free renewable energy is exhausted - less money in a year than a premiership footballer earns. Not to mention the £70 billion (£70,000 million) costs of decommissioning the existing old nuclear power stations or the billions to wreck Iraq - what was that about catastrophe?

Saturday 25th June

We had a booking yesterday for two double rooms so were expecting two couples. When the four guests arrived, however, we were greeted by three young men and a young woman. If the two guys sharing a double room had been a gay couple we would not have had any qualms, but it was made clear that they were only 'straight' friends sharing a bed because no twins were available. Now would our prejudice against groups of men staying together in the B&B be validated?

This morning, before even reaching their rooms to service, I was met by a fire extinguisher blocking the landing with its safety catch broken and half the pressure gone from inside. The apprehension already existing immediately turned into rage.

'Does someone want to explain this to me?' I shouted as I banged loudly on both rooms, opening the doors in the process.

The couple were out, along with one of the single men. The one remaining male was lying in bed looking bedraggled.

'Do you want to tell me what my fire extinguisher is doing **here** and why it is not over **there** with its safety catch on?'

'Oh sorry, my mate in there (pointing to the other room) was messing around with it last night when we got back.'

'Messing around with it? This isn't some idiot student halls of residence. This is my house you're staying in as a guest. And "messing around" with fire extinguishers is a serious health and safety issue. What happens if there is a fire that can't be put out because some wanker has sprayed the extinguisher everywhere for a laugh?'

'Oh no mate. He wasn't spraying about. He just moved it.'

'Why is the catch broken then with half the pressure gone? I've got a good mind you know to just ask you all to leave now.'

'Honestly he wasn't spraying it around. We wouldn't do that. He was pissed right out his box and was just being a bit stupid.'

'Just "pissed right out of his box" - that's alright then hey? Well I'm going to think about this and will be talking to your "mate" when he comes back.'

With exemplary timing, exactly as I reached the bottom of the stairs, all three of the others walked in the door.

'Do want to explain what was going on with the fire extinguisher last night,' I immediately barked at them.

'Sorry? 'Fire extinguishers? What do you mean?'

'So you weren't messing around with the fire extinguishers last night?'

'None of us were, no.'

'Well, that's interesting. Because your "mate" upstairs has just told me how you came back "pissed out of your box" and were messing around.'

'Erm .. Well .. Err .. Well, yeh, we may have moved them a bit but we weren't spraying them around or anything.'

'I'm telling you now. If there is any more "messing around" of whatever type you will all be leaving this house early.'

If absolutely sure the extinguishers had been sprayed they would have all left immediately. As it was I gave them the benefit of doubt which was followed ten minutes later by a knock on the door and a humble apology for 'our unacceptable behaviour.'

Sunday 26th June

Call me a wimp if you like, but it's amazing how heavy quilts can be when changing, especially lots of superking size ones. I've noticed that my arm and shoulder muscles have become reasonably developed, solely from shaking out quilts. Who needs to spend hours in the gym? It's the same with going up and down five flights of stairs constantly, often carrying baskets/vacuum cleaner and luggage - much better for toning the legs and bum than the gym 'stairwalker' machine. So there you go, running a B&B can be good for your health – just go easy on eating all the leftovers from the cooked breakfasts every morning?

Monday 27th June

Two male work colleagues are in Brighton on business. One of the men is very skinny, the other a fair bit over-weight. The first morning at breakfast the skinny guy ordered 'just toast and cereal.' The overweight man then ordered exactly the same but seemed to say it rather reluctantly as he enviously glanced over at someone else's full cooked breakfast. The same scenario repeated itself for the first four days of their stay until this morning when the overweight one came down alone because his work colleague had just checked out.

'Oh, could I have the full English breakfast this morning, please?' he sheepishly asked. 'I have a very busy day ahead of me today so will need something substantial.'

'Of course. No problem.'

When the breakfast was served, once more, he felt the need to qualify and justify his order.

'I wouldn't normally eat a cooked breakfast in the morning but I probably won't get the chance to eat again until late so this [breakfast] will be good for me. Thank you.'

Don't worry. Enjoy it. Stop feeling guilty. One cooked breakfast in five days away on some boring training course isn't bad. If it was me it would have been five consecutive cooked breakfasts. Come to think of it, actually, with leftovers every day it is probably about 350 days a year anyway when I 'treat' myself to some fatty food – occupational hazard is my excuse.

Tuesday 28th June

'Bear with me chap. It's a bit awkward getting the credit card out of the wallet whilst driving one's Mercedes along the A30,' said a *retired colonel* type as he phoned up from his car to make a booking.

Is there any law against booking a B&B/hotel room whilst driving your car? Or perhaps for hoteliers to not accept, like publicans being socially and legally responsible in serving additional alcohol to drunks? Luckily, as horns were bibbing in the background and the *colonel* was muttering 'bloody hells,' there was no crash as he gave his details.

Wednesday 29th June

At 9pm last night, whilst merrily relaxing in the lounge with no further arrivals due, Helen and I both turned to each other as we suddenly heard extremely heavy foot-steps come thundering down the stairs. A few seconds later, and also following the noisy crash of the second floor fire door which vibrated the whole house as it was slammed through, there was a loud and aggressive knock on the lounge door. The indignant man standing there was a guest from the top floor.

'We've got absolutely no hot water in our room and my girlfriend has just had to have a cold shower,' he snapped.

'Oh. That's strange. We keep the boiler on constantly for tap hot water and all the showers are electric so work off a cold-feed anyhow. I'll come and have a look for you,' I replied, ignoring his abruptness, and hoping it was going to be a 'guest being dippy' problem rather than anything more serious.

His girlfriend, when we make it back up to their room, is sitting on the side of the bed with a just a towel around her and also looking displeased. Going into the en suite bathroom, I immediately see that the shower temperature dial is turned fully onto the cold setting. Turning the shower on and the setting up from one to ten, hot water immediately starts to come through.

'There you go, it's working fine. You just had the dial round the wrong way.'

'Well it definitely wasn't working before,' the man again curtly responded still not letting go of the disgruntled tone.

'Look, the water is boiling. You can see steam coming off. The thin, pointed end of the dial needs to be turned to the highest setting.'

'Well that's a bit stupid isn't it? You would think it would be the thick end of the dial you turn.'

At this point I wanted to reply with my own honest feelings:

'No, you are a bit stupid, not the shower. And, next time, before you go slamming around and banging doors and being hostile to people, try and use your brain first. Perhaps, for instance, you could have experimented with the dial in the middle to see if that gave lukewarm not freezing cold water?'

Instead, however, I just politely left them alone. Although, before leaving, I did offer to show how the hot and cold water on the sink tap worked.

Thursday 30th June

There was a large political rally in the city today to protest against the vulnerability of cyclists on the road and also against oil dependence. In true Brighton style, however, the protest took the form of a 'naked bike ride' around the city. Hundreds took part and we were greeted to the sight of much naked flesh and fanfare as the route went by the road adjacent to the B&B. It put a smile on most people's faces, including our new neighbours who rushed back inside to get their cameras out.

JULY

Lesbians and tomatoes

Friday 1st July

A fact for any boffs who are interested in Brighton's cultural history. When ABBA won the Eurovision song contest in 1974 with their lovely hit song *Waterloo* it took place here at the Brighton Dome.

Saturday 2nd July

There is a large cheerleading contest this weekend and Brighton is overrun with hundreds of girls (from three to thirty) in town, mainly accompanied by their mums. The event started early so most of our guests attending the contest missed breakfast apart from one mum who came into the dining room with her eyes rolling.

'I've just dropped her off at the [Brighton] Centre. She's eighteen now and at university but I do still worry about her and what she gets up to. She phoned me up a few weeks after first leaving, all excited, to tell me she has joined a "university society." Great, I first thought, some healthy academic interest where she can meet some interesting new friends. And then she tells me it's the cheerleading society! I couldn't believe it. To be fair to her though it's not as bad as it first sounds. I've since found out that modern cheerleading is much more about gymnastics and dance choreography rather than just being a "ditzy girl with pom poms."'

Sunday 3rd July

The cheerleading contest mum came down alone again for breakfast only this time because 'teenage daughters don't do breakfast.' After actually experiencing the competition the mum has decided that she's not so keen on cheerleading after all.

'I did enjoy seeing my daughter but staying all day was a bit ghastly really. Some of the young girls are barely out of nappies and the mums are unbelievable. Chasing around constantly after their little princesses to top up their blusher and glitter.'

Monday 4th July

How many people are able to change wiper blades for car windscreens? I would like to know because I had to resort to paying Halford's a couple of quid today to get some youngster to do it for me. A rather emasculating experience but necessary, unfortunately, as a fruitless twenty minutes had been spent in the shop's car park with no success. It would be reassuring to know that a large number of other people also find the thirty second operation a bit frustrating?

Tuesday 5th July

The Kemp Town area of Brighton has a free weekly news-paper which is put together by some local volunteers. Being the 'Gay Village' it quite often has a diverse range of topics including an article this week highlighting how gay men on average earn more than the general population and also punch above their weight in the creative industries. Now not wanting to necessarily put an obstinate downer on the creative and money-making genius of gay men, but is it more the case that not having kids is the bigger factor? How do the average figures stack up when compared to straight people who have not spent hundreds of thousands bringing little angels up? And all the time and energy spent dealing with the child-rearing malarkey as well - not exactly conducive to stimulating the creative flow, being knackered all the time ("I was going to write that bestseller but haven't had any sleep for three months and also changed ten smelly nappies today.")

Regardless, if kids do cause ambitions to be relinquished and relative poverty, it does not validate child abuse - be honest parents, the odds of success were always unlikely anyway and at least now you have a good excuse for failure. View your children instead as a creative process and, by pushing all your past competitive dreams (frustrations) on to them, it will help the evolutionary development of the human race. Or perhaps just lead to another generation laden with the psychological neurosis of their parents?

Wednesday 6th July

It is not very often we have guests arrive straight from the airport having just flown in from Afghanistan. Today, however, a youngish couple working for the Department of International Development checked in from their usual base in Kabul helping with the reconstruction of the country.

'How does it feel arriving back in Britain? It must be quite a contrast to Afghanistan?'

'Slightly surreal. It's certainly a very different world.'

'And is it a dangerous environment to work in?'

'Well you obviously have to be extremely security conscious and we always receive a lot of military back-up and protection, but Kabul is a lot different to other areas of the country. It's a lot more dangerous outside the capital, especially in the southern areas.'

Wow. If you really are that fed-up with the office job it's not just running a B&B you can do. Why not go to work in Afghanistan? That should provide some adrenaline. Helping with development is probably fairly useful as well.

Thursday 7th July

A company from 'up north' booked a double room for one of their employees. Yesterday a man in his mid-twenties turned up for the reservation who seemed ok, apart perhaps from the over-styled silly haircut. This morning, however, when we went to change the room after check-out we discovered (instantly from the overpowering stench of stale urine as soon as we opened the door) that the employee had wet the bed. Now was this just an unfortunate accident or was it socially unacceptable behaviour, especially as we knew the young man (with the silly haircut) had been out drinking heavily? Helen had the latter view and wanted to instantly phone up the company to let everyone know that their work colleague 'pee's the bed when drunk.' Although I considered that humiliating someone at their workplace was probably a little harsh, it took a lot of self-control not to phone as I stripped resentfully the urine drenched sheets and mattress protectors.

Friday 8th July

Last night on TV was another 'Top Hundred' of all time variation show, this one the greatest music videos ever. Despite an aversion to Nick Hornbyesque style 'lists' generally, at least such programmes can give some useful ideas when an annoying git asks you to name your 'top five.' Anyhow, today I was in our local deli when the person serving me acknowledged another customer that walked in.

'Oh, hello there. How are things? I saw you on TV last night. Where were you on the list, number thirty something, not bad heh?'

Of course, being nosey, I was intrigued to know what 'famous' person was standing next to me. However, after a few minutes of less than surreptitious side glances, I still could not place who the mystery music star was? Then, and to save me from any loitering shame after already being served, the truth was revealed. Kevin Rowland from *Dexys Midnight Runners*! So many memories of dancing round to 'Come on Eileen' at school discos and weddings and now, here we are together, ordering lunch. If only I had put my dungarees on this morning.

Saturday 9th July

Kemp Town often reminds me of the TV advert a few years ago for a certain brand of continental lager, which showed a various eclectic assortment of 'alternative' Dutch characters shopping in a supermarket. In our local store today were a group of three transvestites (slightly towards the style of *Little Britain's*, 'But I'm a lady'), happily minding their own business with no one batting an eyelid. The already cosmopolitan mix, of course, could not really care less. How many other supermarkets in the country could a group of transvestites shop together without any hassle?

Sunday 10th July

A young Spanish couple, planning on living in Brighton for a year, booked only through email because they were too 'scared to phone and speak English.' Since arriving yesterday the conversation has been mostly in Spanish, which we speak to a very limited degree, and the couple apparently 'need' to find both a job and a house quickly because they have 'no much' money.

'You phone for us, please,' the couple said today, holding up some ringed entries from the property rental section of the local paper.

Although throwing yourself fully in the deep end is the best away to learn a language, a little assistance to find somewhere first to live probably helps. Not sure if I'm expected to find them a job though as well?

Monday 11th July

'Sorry about the weather,' I said to a Norwegian guest. 'It doesn't normally rain constantly for a whole week in summer.'

'There's no such thing as bad weather, only bad clothes,' was the reply.

True, really. If cloud and rain are always viewed as 'bad' weather and 'depressing' then living in Britain could only be a miserable experience regardless for much of the time.

Tuesday 12th July

'We're here to escape the bloody kids for a few days. They've been driving us nuts.'

'Don't worry. You're not alone. A good chunk of our guests seem to stay for exactly the same reason. Either that or "to escape London." How old are the kids anyhow?'

'Well good question. That's exactly the point really. I wouldn't mind if they were youngsters but they're all in their thirties now! That's the problem these days; house prices are so expensive you get stuck living with your kids for life. I sometimes think we're never going to get rid them. We're even thinking about going away for a week at Christmas - just the two of us - to get some time out.'

I wonder whether the 'kids' feel exactly the same way about having to still live with their parents but just can't afford to do anything about it?

Wednesday 13th July

Four middle aged men pay £12 each to watch the cricket at the Sussex county ground in Brighton when most of the day is a complete washout because of rain.

'We only got to see five overs so it cost us £2.40 an over or 40p for every ball - That's cricket though in an English summer I guess.'

Thursday 14th July

Normally when people order breakfasts they do not pick and choose off the menu, just ask for the 'full English' and then leave the plate with leftovers - the healthy grilled tomatoes usually. In the last few weeks, however, we have had four separate consecutive lesbian couples stay who have specifically requested in advance, 'full English please but no tomatoes.' Is this statistically significant or only a mere coincidence? What are the chances of four in a row of a specific group all separately ordering exactly the same rarely asked for request? Now, please, do not shoot the messenger. I am only reporting on an observed factual occurrence which probably implies nothing about the healthiness of lesbian eating habits. Maybe lesbians just care more about not wasting food unnecessarily?

Friday 15th July

Another interesting observation, on the subject of the eating habits of specific groups, is the high percentage of guests from an Afro-Caribbean background who request their fried eggs to be 'flipped over' to make sure the yolk is very well cooked. If it is a distinct cultural preference passed down it shows how the ingrained habits of forebears can endure on strongly – or at least for a few generations. Similar perhaps to how many Australians still have a culture of eating heavy Sunday roasts even when it is forty degrees Celsius outside.

Saturday 16th July

A shy couple, staying in the room with the now irksome electric macerator, knocked gingerly on the lounge door today looking very awkward and embarrassed.

'Do you have a plunger we could borrow? Our toilet is blocked up. We've only put tissue down it, honestly, no objects. We saw the notice [requesting no sanitary items, condoms, cotton buds etc are flushed] in the bathroom.'

'That's ok. Sorry for the inconvenience. We know the toilet can sometimes block up regardless. I'll come up and fix it for you.'

'It's ok honest,' the man responded again sheepishly. 'It's awfully mucky and not very pleasant.'

'Don't worry. I'm used to dealing with all sorts running this place. It's part of the job.'

Perhaps though it would have been better to let them sort out the problem themselves? As I donned the marigolds and cleared the aptly described 'unpleasant' blockage, the couple hovered in the background obviously flustered and in discomfit at someone else seeing their personal 'mess.' Fair enough. It's not really the ideal scenario you want when enjoying a romantic weekend away with your partner. Personally I was just happy to get the toilet fixed without calling out an expensive plumber.

Anyhow, we are going on holiday ourselves tomorrow, so have a few days off to forget about such matters.

And if our hotel toilet blocks up we will gladly and unabashedly let someone else sort it out!

Saturday 23rd July

Helen's brother got married in the medieval Tuscan town where he had proposed to his now wife, so we have just been to their wedding. A good excuse to get away as we would not have gone otherwise - being nervous still about the finances in running a new business. A break was probably much needed after working seven days a week constantly since we started - all work and no play after all makes you a bit dull.

Holiday pay, however, does not exist when you are self-employed and the large mortgage millstone soon makes you nervous again. When closing a B&B you also lose overflow bookings for the two-three days either side of a break, and future reservations, so time off quickly becomes expensive in lost earnings. Some people do employ relief managers but this can be more stressful than worthwhile.

Having new guests arrive the day after a holiday should not be problematic. However, when a flight is repeatedly delayed and you are stuck in Pisa airport through the night, the return then becomes rather more anxious. And even more so when the last coach/trains to Brighton have stopped running when you do finally get to Gatwick at 5am. Next time we have a holiday it would be more prudent to leave a day buffer in case of any unforeseen delays – it is probably best to not have new guests waiting on your doorstep when you first arrive back.

Sunday 24th July

There has been lots of discussion recently on the radio and in the newspapers about the crisis in housing and government subsidised schemes to specifically help 'key workers' - mainly state-sector professionals - to afford to buy their own homes. What about all the supposed non-key workers though? Where are they supposed to live, or do they not count? All the low wage workers stacking our food and on the check-outs in supermarkets, or the bus driver taking us to work, or those picking up the litter on the streets - are not all these jobs an essential key also for life to run smoothly? Most of the B&B's/hotels in Brighton would probably struggle if there was nowhere to buy food supplies from, no transport for guests to arrive on, and a city knee-deep in litter because no one was employed to clear it up. Of course, workers to do these jobs will always be found, but surely these people deserve to afford their own housing as well?

Monday 25th July

Since my musings yesterday I have been imagining that some Blimp has been scoffing at such 'radical' views - a counterargument something along the lines of 'people in low paid manual jobs should have worked harder at school and governments also should not interfere with the *free* market.'

Is it not a fallacy of composition to argue that people in low paid manual jobs completely deserve their lot? If everyone came from the 'perfect' aspirational family and *all* kids had gone to university – would *all* find them-selves graduate/professional jobs? Low paid manual jobs would still exist - just that workers then would be university educated. A more erudite society - 'education, education, education' etc may be desirable - but 'key' workers regardless are required for the vast majority of jobs, not just a few select professions.

And surely only the seriously delusional still believe in the magical workings of the 'free' market – that markets are independently functioning entities that naturally create a harmonious equilibrium. Inasmuch as markets are institutions which are embedded in a social and polit-ical framework that can vary, the government can inter-vene to create a much more favourable outcome - aren't affordable housing and 'fair wage' employment supposed to be a basic human right?

Tuesday 26th July

Nothing too exciting has happened again in the B&B today so I've been fantasising about being like the Duke of Westminster who owns hundreds of acres of Mayfair and Belgravia. Once you have control of such prime free-hold riches you can't go wrong really. Just sit back (with your descendents) and take the monopoly rent forever. Nice work if you can get it.

In Brighton there are 150,000 dwellings with an aver-age price of £300,000 - a total housing stock worth £45 billion. If you were a multi-billionaire you could buy up every house. Wouldn't that be great, I would own the whole city and title myself the 'Duke of Brighton.'

Wednesday 27th July

A piece of information about (my) fiefdom of Brighton incidentally is that elm trees are dominant in the city (30,000 of them, including a famous one in the Royal Pavilion gardens) and it was one of the few areas in the whole of Britain to escape the Dutch Elm disease scourge of the 1970's. Apparently the beetles that cause and spread the disease are not actually great travellers and could not make the tough climb over the South Downs leaving Brighton and a thin strip of the south coast protected.

Thursday 28th July

A very idiosyncratically English couple - in a sort of 'Mr Bean' way - are always wearing matching socks, sandals and anoraks. This morning at breakfast, when the dining room was full of other guests, the matching clothes theme continued with a slight twist when both came in wearing nothing else but a swimming costume and trunks of similar design and pattern. The bemused gaze of all the other guests was probably enhanced also by the woman being somewhat overweight and the swimming costume ill-fittingly small. Furthermore, the couple both had lobster-red sunburnt shoulders.

'We're going straight down the beach after breakfast. But I think we'd better use factor six sun cream today because yesterday we used factor five and we both got really burnt.'

'Perhaps you should try some factor thirty with sunburn like that.'

'Oh no. I'm sure we'll be ok with one whole extra factor.'

Friday 29th July

A Swedish chef has now been staying with us for a couple of weeks, paid by his employers, until more permanent long-term accommodation becomes available (and, yes, he has heard joke references before to *The Muppet Show*). For those with any doubt I can vouch that chefs do work extremely hard for their money. Aside, of course, from working in a hot kitchen environment and being under pressure to produce quality food to tight deadlines, there is also the long hours involved. Our Swedish friend seems permanently knackered from working both a long early and late shift every day, catching only a few disjointed hours break in between - apparently such conditions being the norm in the industry. Ok if you are an owner-chef who gets to take the profits home otherwise it appears literally a bit of a 'sweat shop' job. The waiting staff are probably better paid with all those cash tips. Surely it's more skilful to prepare and cook food than to serve it? I can just imagine every time a chef hears from a waiter/waitress that a customer 'sends their compliments' what they really want to reply is - 'well give us some of the tip then.'

Saturday 30th July

Two women in their mid-twenties arrived late on a hot humid summer night. When I opened the door to show them into the room it felt nice and refreshingly cool because I had forgot to close the windows earlier after fully opening them to give a good airing.

'Ooh, how lovely. The room has air conditioning as well,' one of them exclaimed in mistake for the slight breeze that was blowing through the room.

'Sorry to disappoint but we don't have air conditioning. It's just that the windows are wide open,' I felt obliged to inform them.

Sunday 31st July

Sometimes people do ask for something in a more long-winded way than necessary.

'Yes, I think I would like to have the full cooked breakfast option, but not the beans … nor the hash brown … or tomatoes … or the bacon … and no sausage please either.'

'So you would just like a fried egg then?'

'Yes, just one fried egg please.'

AUGUST

Are you a "Catty" or a "Protty?"

Monday 1st August

Overhearing sex antics in B&Bs/hotels is a cliché of course but nevertheless a true occurrence. When you live in a B&B and have a private bedroom below a guest room you inevitably get 'disturbed' also by people 'enjoying' their holiday.

'I'd like to book a room at the single occupancy rate for six nights please.

I may also have a friend stay for a few of the days. Would it be ok, if my friend does stay, to only pay the full double rate for those nights?' a young woman had asked a few weeks ago.

No problem. Nice long booking. And, if mostly single occupancy, the room above us would be ideal - single people generally being quieter than couples.

On the first night the woman was alone and we hardly heard a sound from the room. However, on the second and third nights, she did indeed 'have' a friend and we were kept awake for hours each night by the noisy groans and bed squeaking of lovemaking with her female companion. No real big drama, not the first time we have overheard such goings on, but interestingly we have been treated to the same repeat virtuoso perform-ance for the previous two nights also. The twist in the tale, though, is that the female friend was swapped on these last two nights for a male companion - obviously eclectic sexual preferences to go along with the stamina. We are just intrigued now as to what noises will come our way tonight and who will turn up at breakfast tomorrow morning?

Tuesday 2ⁿᵈ August

Sorry, no more exciting exploits to report. The woman quietly went back to single occupancy, had breakfast alone and checked out this morning - although she did have a smile on her face incidentally as she left.

Wednesday 3ʳᵈ August

Are sales people all just an odious, commission obsessed bunch with no morals or do they provide a valuable service which informs people of previously unknown consumer possibilities? Today, following a telephone sales call earlier, a 'no obligation' photographer turned up to discuss options for new business cards.

'Right,' as soon as the photographer stepped foot in the door, 'let me take some photos for you and get a *deal* worked out *today*. We can get you a good price. You look like a man who knows how to do a *deal*.'

'Well, I'm just after a quote at the moment, thank you.'

'Don't worry. We'll be able to sort things out *today*. We produce great business cards. Here, have a look at these examples we have done for other B&Bs. Lovely quality. You can have whatever design you want. *Today* we'll do a *deal* and we can offer the best prices.'

As this same patter continued throughout the process of taking sample photos of the rooms I could not help thinking of *Derren Brown* and how sales people use similar tactics (conscious or not) of 'psychology, suggestion and misdirection.' In the end the constant assertive bombardment of the words 'deal' and 'today' were too much to bear.

'Look, I appreciate these photos being taken and will consider the packages you're offering, but *today* I will not be signing up to any *deal*. I will be getting at least one other quote for comparison before making any decision.'

'Well, we can only offer these prices if you sign up *today*. Otherwise it's going to be a lot more expensive for you. These different *deals* I'm offering *today* won't be available at a later date.'

Aaarrggghh. They're odious. Not nice like I previously thought. Be warned, especially if you ever invite these sales people directly into your house, they will not take no for an answer and will try to 'close the deal' (to use their speak) at all costs on the appointment. I think they all use the some 1970s double glazing style direct sales training manual as their 'Guide to the Hard Sell' bible. And, of course, the same deals are always available, even at a better rate, if you go back later.

Thursday 4th August

'We're really tempted actually to buy another property in Morocco. The market offers a fantastic potential return - yield and capital growth - and only three hours flight. Why bother with Spain? The property bubble has completely burst there,' was a conversation overheard at breakfast this morning.

Globalisation is quite a boon for those already with capital, especially as the same free movement privilege is not extended to labour in the global marketplace. And given that emerging markets are also so far behind in the capital accumulation stakes would it not be possible for the rich to get a virtual monopoly on all the prime property in the world before the poor get a look in? The rich billion could be the equivalent of the Duke of Westminster in Belgravia. What a potential scenario - a billion buy-to-let landlords living off the rent of the other six billion workers. Whole countries could earn their living in the global economy solely from being rentiers.

Friday 5th August

Most men would probably be flattered to be propositioned by an attractive blond woman?

Kemp Town, because it's Gay Pride weekend, is closed to traffic. All the deli's and restaurants have extra seating out on the streets and lots of people are milling around in the sunshine enjoying the atmosphere. Approaching the corner deli earlier, near to the B&B on St James's street, I suddenly noticed a pretty blond woman sitting with a man, looking at me intently. After a few seconds eye contact, however, and not recognizing her, I carried on to the B&B whilst she still stared after me. Thirty minutes later the doorbell rang and the male companion of the blond woman was standing there with a card envelope, addressed to 'Man in Black Jacket.'

'I'm so sorry for disturbing you but my friend wanted you to have this,' he said, with a camp accent, as he handed me the envelope.

The card inside had a cowboy on the front with a human size cockerel adjacent and a caption that read:

'This man has a huge cock.'

Inside it was handwritten:

'If you're on your own - I am too. Lets do something mad together. Do I know you, are you my dentist? Katy, [her phone number] xxx.'

It suddenly dawned on me, of course, that 'Katy' would have been one of the many dolled up drag queens that are very common on Pride weekend. The rest of the year, when it's mainly just your normal transvestites in Kemp Town, it is far easier to spot them as men (sorry guys but it's true). Some of the 'women' in drag however are much more convincing. Very confusing. What does 'are you my dentist' mean as well?

Saturday 6th August

Is consenting sex between adults not a private matter? We visited the 'Gay Pride' festival site, just to know what it was all about and join in the celebrations (although not 'know' in the biblical sense, honest.) Anyhow, after the colourful parade of floats/costumes/music etc has been through the city centre it makes its way to a designated park where everybody gathers for a further afternoon of carnival. As we approached the park, however, there was a group of Christian protestors which, in somewhat spoiling the atmosphere of tolerance and goodwill, served to highlight perhaps why it is still necessary for such parades to take place. This sanctimonious bunch of zealots somehow felt justified to picket the park entrance with loud hailers announcing various insulting chants:

'Homosexuality is evil ... Sodomites will burn in hell ... Crimes against god ...'

The festival goers did not seem too unduly worried and rather good-naturedly just ignored the protestors.

For those that did challenge, it was mostly humorous retorts rather than outright confrontation:

'Just give us a kiss, darling. Go on. One little kiss for Pride.'

Or slightly more provocative.

'Go stick your religion up your arse.'

Imagine if these religious extremists were ever to get into power? Where would it stop? Heterosexuals would probably follow also in the line of fire:

'Use <u>only</u> the missionary position or you will burn in hell ... Sex only for reproduction reasons, <u>no</u> enjoyment.'

And what about the practicalities of enforcement - would there be 'Ministry for Religious Sex Police' web cams in all bedrooms? Surely such policies though are never going to be great vote winners?

Sunday 7th August

Yesterday a conservative looking German couple with two children aged ten and twelve had turned up for an advanced booking not realising it was Gay Pride weekend. The family also looked particularly bemused because the 'colourful' spectacle of the Parade was in full flow when they first arrived. Furthermore the family is in two rooms on the front of the house which directly over-looks one of the music stages for the street party that has still not stopped going.

'It was a very interesting night,' said the Germans at breakfast this morning, in a room full with Pride guests.

Apparently the music stages and street party this year are much bigger and louder than ever before and literally tens of thousands were packed outside the B&B, only

really quieting down slightly between 5am and 9am.
Probably not the exact summer holiday the Germans had
planned but they were in jovial spirits anyhow and, why
not, they had some of the best seats in Kemp Town.

Monday 8th August

Loosely connected to religion and sex is a new theory of
mine to perhaps help explain, and potentially counteract, terrorism – it's called the 'Masturbate for World
Peace' theory. A nature documentary recently showed
young adult male monkeys with severe signs of distress
whenever they witnessed the alpha male mating with a
female. All of the young adult males, in their celibate
frustration, would scamper to the top of different trees
and ferociously shake the branches back and forth whilst
howling painfully out loud.

Now obviously there is the small matter of human
evolutionary progress over monkeys, but the parallels of
sexually frustrated young human males in today's society are clear to see. Is pub closing time not a painful and
distressful site to witness - for the anthropological
observer as well as many of the young men? At least,
though, in our largely secular and sexually liberated
world many young people are either busy actually
sowing their wild oats or alternatively masturbating furi-
ously. But, and this is the key to the new theory, the strict
religious people are left to suffer like our poor young
monkey cousins - hormones raging and without any
form of sexual release. Quite clearly it is a recipe for
disaster and can lead to people wanting to blow themselves and others up. If you also add in other minor

factors such as political injustice, poverty and unemployment, the theory seems to be even more valid?

Tuesday 9th August

The punk-folk band *The Levellers* are apparently from
and still based in Kemp Town, with their own recording
studio also just round the corner. At *Glastonbury* in the
days when 'crusties' and 'new age travellers' were far
more prevalent (you know, 'the glory pre-corporate
days, when you could break-in for free') I remember
being excited to see *The Levellers* headline. Anyhow,
walking past a group of dreadlocked new age travellers
with a couple of obligatory crustie dogs at that time, one
of them brusquely shouted out at me.

'Give us a swig of that beer.'

The request was ignored due to the overt hostility and
unsolicited condescension for me obviously not being
'crustie' enough.

'Fuck off then, you indie kid wanker.'

Amazing how a certain breed of 'hippie' only seems to
have free love and goodwill towards people they perceive
as 'alternative' as themselves. Without the attitude and
rudeness (and, to be honest, the bad breath as well)
I would have gladly shared a beer. It's always been an
additional irony as well that such hardcore anti-capital-
ist eco-warriors used to travel extensively as a way of life
in battered old large polluting vans. Very 'green' not too
mention the hypocritical fact that an eco-anarchist society would never be able to produce such industrial
goods, especially the latest efficient technologies - who's
being parasitic on who?

Wednesday 10th August

Not sure whether it is a normal Japanese custom but four guests from Tokyo have each left a pound coin for us every day, one on each pillow. If a tip is supposed to make you feel warmer and more amenable towards guests it certainly works - in fact, Helen and me have both been rushing up early in the morning to be the first to service their rooms (finders keepers is our rule on tips.)

In Tokyo apparently it is the norm now to have hi-tech electronic 'turbo toilets' that are paperless with an automatic built-in bidet service. Supposedly once one of these modern toilets has been experienced it feels a bit 'unclean' when going back to just using a normal 'bog' standard toilet. Such hi-tech advances, however, have got me slightly concerned about whether our Japanese guests are sufficiently satisfied with the facilities here. How to phrase the question though? Is there a polite way of asking someone whether their bum is clean enough?

Thursday 11th August

'I'm middle class now because I store my coal in the bidet,' John Prescott has reportedly said.

If he can dispense with the separate bidet does that mean that he also now has a fancy electronic 'turbo' dryer toilet? There's an image to picture.

Friday 12th August

Two English couples were having a conversation at breakfast this morning.

'... I just didn't expect a few drinks back at Liam's to end up being so confrontational. The guy was acting like such a prick. We were all just talking normally about how things are now in Belfast and he kept interrupting in a really aggressive manner.'

'So what are yiz, a Catty [Catholic] or a Protty [Protestant]?' the man relating the story continued, mimicking a heavy Northern Irish accent.

'We just all carried on and tried to ignore the bloke but he said it again and again. "So what are yiz then, a Catty or a Protty?" I couldn't believe it. Honestly thought it was going to kick off. Liam apologised for him later when he left. Said he's a real hardcore nationalist nutcase. And only a friend of a friend.'

How many generations more before the sectarian divide is history?

Saturday 13th August

A young research student who stayed with us last night after attending a conference at the University of Sussex was sharing his concerns with me today over his PhD project.

'I'm two years into it now and don't feel like I've made any progress. If anything I'm more confused now than when I started,' he told me in a dejected tone.

'Don't worry everyone feels like that at first. Keep going and eventually things will all click into place,' I tried to offer reassurance.

'Hope so, otherwise it will have been a complete a waste of time.'

If being more honest, of course, I would have told him that some people spend their whole lives pursuing a project only to realise they have been on completely the wrong track. Perhaps it's the journey that is the most important thing though?

Sunday 14th August

Whilst standing on the outside step today of one of the (gay) neighbours, having a perfectly normal conversation, a slobby white guy in his late thirties waddled towards us with an intent stare of disdain.

'Bloody faggots,' he muttered as he walked past.

'Got a problem?' the neighbour inquired when he continued the sneering hostile look.

'Fuck off,' was the less than intelligible response.

'You really need to come to terms with your latent homosexuality,' I said to the slobby buffoon. 'Being in such denial is making you very uptight. It's not healthy.'

Not sure whether the wind-up comment was quite understood but he did not seem to see the funny side regardless as he walked off muttering additional expletives.

'Ah, I'm not worried by him,' the neighbour casually remarked. 'I've seen and heard a lot worse. When you're not even allowed to go to your sister's wedding because her fella doesn't like "poofs" you're not going to let someone like him get to you.'

Monday 15th August

Apparently the street our B&B is in used to be called 'German Place' but the name was patriotically changed when World War Two started. Maybe that explains why the street escaped bomb damage whereas other parts of Kemp Town were flattened?

Tuesday 16ᵗʰ August

'I guess you must get to see a good cross-section of people in your job,' I said when meeting up with my accountant today. 'Do you have many interesting clients?'

'Yes, many,' she said laughing. 'I certainly never thought I would be doing the books for a Dominatrix. That's Brighton for you though.'

I'm sure, however, there are Dominatrixes in every town and city (and village?) in the country?

Wednesday 17ᵗʰ August

There are two young American girls staying in a twin room but only one came down to breakfast. Later on I saw the other girl, who passed me rather apprehensively on the stairs with an equally looking nervous young man.

'Oh, this is my friend. He just lives here.'

'Lives *here* in the B&B?'

'I mean he lives here in Brighton. Not *here*.'

Soon after I serviced their room and there were three backpacks, one of them clearly with male clothes. There was also a condom packet on the side and used condoms in the bin.

'Do you want to tell me the truth about how many people are staying in your room?' I later asked.

'He did stay over last night but it's not what you think. We didn't plan in the first place for there to be three of us … We're really sorry.'

Not the biggest crime in the world but we don't really want strangers being brought back to the house. It is a B&B after all not a backpackers or a student halls of residence. Still, having cottoned on to the sneaking in, at least we were able to charge the guy for the privilege of sleeping over.

Thursday 18th August

'Cor, I was so hot last night,' a middle aged male guest said to me this morning. 'She [thumb gesture towards his partner] always thinks it's cold no matter what though. Wouldn't let me open the windows right up. No need really for a quilt in this heat. Not for me anyway.'

Many similar comments have also been made in the past by other guests and it is normally females who prefer the room temperature and bedding to be warmer? Whether any gender bias exists, or not, it seems that views either way can diverge quite widely in relation to what constitutes a pleasant sleeping environment. If we were a really trendy boutique establishment we would offer a choice of custom made quilts stitched into two halves – perhaps four and a half togs on one side for men, fifteen togs on the other for women?

Friday 19th August

Russia has just invaded Georgia so Thomas Friedman's *Golden Arches Theory of Conflict Prevention*, which argued that countries with *McDonalds* have never gone to war with each other, has at least one conflict now to disprove it (too much to lose apparently from globalisation and economic interdependence.) The theory was always a load of 'Kroc' in the first place though.

Saturday 20th August

A 'New Agey' type woman guest was talking away generally today (about something or the other ...) when she said:

'Oh I know things will be alright because I have my spirit guide looking over me. He's a North American Indian chief.'

How come 99% of spirit guides are North American Indians when they have never constituted more than 1% of the world's population? What is the secret to their spiritual monopoly over all other ethnic groups?

Sunday 21st August

There is much talk in the media, following the EU's recent expansion to incorporate Eastern European countries, of a 'flood' of new foreign arrivals. This is touted as especially so for the UK because France, Germany and others had implemented restrictions to prevent hoards of 'Polish plumbers' from 'stealing' all the jobs. Leaving aside the debate about the relative merits of immigration, from the anecdotal evidence of running a B&B at this time, there is without doubt a massive influx of people. Every day for months now we have had Eastern

Europeans knocking directly on the door looking for work, sending emails with CVs attached, and phoning up. All the CVs, to give credit, are extremely impressive and most seem to speak about four languages to go with their polite English skills. As Norman Tebbit once said, people 'should get on their bikes' and look for jobs wherever they can find them. In the modern era of globalisation the Eastern Europeans are merely updating this to 'jumping on their nearest budget airline.' In return, of course, for all this labour inflow we get to spend all of our capital buying up their cheap property to use as second homes (well, some of us do anyway.)

Monday 22nd August

It's quite normal for guests to ask for a second key but more so when it is friends in a twin room rather than married couples. Even more odd is when the wife seems to spend most her time alone in the room when the husband often goes out by himself, day and night. An English couple in their fifties arrived a few days ago and from the start we were slightly puzzled by them. She was very shy and a little nervous and he looked like a shave-haired Cockney gangster but who spoke very softly and politely. Things became much clearer today, however, when talking to the neighbours.

'We saw you've got Mr and Mrs Bailey staying with you. Does he go out a lot by himself while she stays back in the room? They always used to stay with us until we bumped into him one night in *Revenge* [a local gay club]. I don't think he saw the funny side when I asked "Does your wife know you're here?"'

Suddenly it seemed obvious. Of course he is gay. Just wonder whether his wife does actually know or not? Perhaps they got married back in the sixties when it was still illegal to be gay and been unable to break out of the double life ever since? I'm sure the Bailey's are not alone, though, especially in the numerous countries worldwide where capital punishment still exists for being homosexual.

Tuesday 23rd August

On the subject of gay cruising, only more out of the closet this time, it was in the tabloid papers recently that George Michael got caught in the act on Hampstead Heath with an unemployed, overweight, fifty-eight year old from Brighton. Now not wanting to be too dispiriting to any straight fifty-eight year old men who are fat and unemployed, but the chances are probably slim of you popping off to your local park and getting a bunk up with Kylie or Madonna.

Wednesday 24th August

Some guests arrived from Paris today having driven their car and taken the ferry to Newhaven, which is a few miles along the coast from Brighton. Looking up the distance, Paris is actually closer to Brighton than Sheffield (Helen's home city.) Although perhaps that is not too surprising really when you take a plane south out of Gatwick and can clearly see the short distance between the French coastline and Brighton.

Whenever other Brits eulogize about how great some place like Australia is and wanting to emigrate it's always comforting to think how lucky we actually are to live in Europe. Both continents are roughly the same size but Australia can't really compete unless you're keen on a sparse population and gum trees. Which has the greater cultural and landscape richness and diversity - London to Paris to Rome to Istanbul, or Perth to Adelaide to Canberra to Sydney? Surely it must be Europe that is the lucky country?

Thursday 25th August

As well as moving to Australia possibly being a bad idea, is 'escaping to the country' not too desirable either? In Brighton there are shops, pubs and restaurants, cinemas, music venues, comedy clubs, theatres, numerous sports clubs and facilities, schools, healthcare, and everything else that the human project has to offer. What has the countryside got apart from a few extra trees and no jobs for your children?

Friday 26th August

Although liking and appreciating the millions of French, Spanish, and Italians etc. just on our doorstep it can be incredibly frustrating for all involved when you don't speak the same language - or perhaps it's just part of the fun? We have Italian guests in at the moment that do not speak any English but who obviously want to still communicate. It's amazing just how long a conversation can go on for when one side is talking Italian and the other English and both don't understand each other's language.

Saturday 27ᵗʰ August

Our plumber has informed us that we need to get a new hot water tank in addition to a new 'efficient' boiler being fitted.

'It's going to cost you though,' he said, in infamous tradesperson speak. 'The price of copper has rocketed in the last year.'

Although, of course, it is inevitable that any trade job 'will cost you' it is actually true that copper along with all other commodities have soared in value in the last year. So much so, in fact, that any two pence piece made before 1992 is actually worth three pence in copper - money, then, that is literally worth less than its own weight.

Sunday 28ᵗʰ August

Amongst the many different conferences that are held in Brighton there are at least three to four quite large reli-gious conferences that take place every year. This week there is a Christian denomination whose members are mainly Caribbean (or of Caribbean descent) and the majority of our rooms are let to people attending the Conference. Now as a secular minded fella who can't really understand how educated people can believe in superstition over science, you might expect that a house full of religious people could be a potentially irksome experience. On the contrary, though, all of our present and past Christian visitors have consistently proved themselves to be some of the most pleasant and trouble-free guests. All of the normal behavioural risks that exist when running a B&B - people being too drunk, noisy, rude, smoking in the rooms etc - are problems that you never usually have to worry about encountering with Christians. Now don't worry, I'm not about to undergo any religious awakening, but perhaps the Richard Dawkins *et al* crowd undermine their own objectives somewhat in the *degree* of their vociferous criticism and uncompromising intolerance of all things superstitious. In the guise of the liberal minded, well-intentioned almost apologetic version of Christianity which exists in this country, maybe it's intellectually counter-productive to be so bellicose towards such people. It could well be true anyway that a significant number of Christians actually agree with a lot of atheist arguments but are unwilling to sacrifice the social and cultural heritage that gives them a sense of community and well being. What is worse - a group of people who seek to live their lives within a moral framework and have a community of singing, music and other shared activities, or a group of wasters who have never once given a second thought to anything ethical and who leave cigarette burns and puke in your rooms?

Monday 29th August

Although a new found awareness that religious people are not simply deluded and barking mad has once more been confirmed this week, would this particular congregation be somewhat less liberal minded than the mainstream Church of England given its close ties to the Caribbean – particularly on the issue of gay rights?

As homosexuality is still illegal in much of the Caribbean, and successful music artists have been famous for lyrics advocating the murder of 'batty boys,' it did cross my mind that the 'love thy neighbour' friendliness of these guests could be rather conditional.

The potential conservatism of our religious congregation was especially interesting, however, because directly above our bedroom we had two female conference guests who had expressly booked 'a double room' and who for the last two nights have kept us awake with their rather noisy lovemaking. Of course, I wanted to ask their views on being both Christian and gay, but thought perhaps it could be a potentially inappropriate and embarrassing question, particularly if the subject was brought up in front of the other guests over breakfast.

Tuesday 30th August

'Complements on your beds - they really are extremely comfortable,' an older gentleman guest said today.

'Talking of beds,' he continued, 'there is a funny story from the days when I worked as a GP before retirement. I had to go once to a house to certify a death whilst the body was still lying there. A chap, poor fella, had a heart attack in bed at home. I was shown into this narrow little bedroom and sat down on the bed because of the lack of space either side.'

'Got the shock of my life,' he carried on roaring with laughter. 'Never realised it was a water bed. The bed sunk straight down and this dead body sprung bolt up to me face to face!'

Wednesday 31st August

A new innovative excuse for binge eating could perhaps have been discovered! This morning a guest ate all his full cooked breakfast, most of his girlfriends (only ordered on his behalf), along with two full racks of toast.

'That should keep you going,' I said when clearing the plates as the man sat back indicating he was full by patting his stomach and sighing.

'I know it seems a bit gluttonous but I've got a theory that if you eat lots of calories all at once you will not get fat because your body can't process an overloaded intake.'

The rather flaky 'wishful thinking' theory seemed to be said in all seriousness. Seeing him pat himself though with all that food inside was so turning my own stomach that I didn't want to stay and argue.

SEPTEMBER

Don't mention the Hitler

Thursday 1st September

George W. Bush was once again brightening up the dining room today with his words of wisdom coming through the radio at breakfast. These latest pearls, even more scary than usual, were made in a direct address to Palestinian ministers.

'I'm driven with a mission from God. God would tell me, "George, go and fight those terrorists in Afghanistan." And I did, and then God would tell me, "George, go and end the tyranny in Iraq" …And I did.'

The most powerful man on the planet decides to wage war because of a supernatural command - aren't people normally sectioned if they hear voices inside their head advocating violence? Also, why did god not bother to tell George that "no weapons of mass destruction" ever existed in the first place?

Friday 2nd September

It probably doesn't help second and third generation immigrants to feel culturally integrated when people often assume their parents/grandparents ethnic background is still dominant.

'Hi Scott,' an Australian guest with a broad Ozzie accent but of Indian appearance asked today. 'I'm looking to do a bit of sightseeing. Could you tell me where the Marina is and how best to get there?'

'Yes, it's about a mile along the seafront going east. Quite a nice walk or you can catch the new *tuc tucs* there now. You know what a *tuc tuc* is don't you? They're those small .... Oh, what am I saying, of course you know what they are ...'

As the assumption trailed off that 'an Indian' evidently knows all about *tuc tucs*, an awkward atmosphere ensued. Or did our guest just assume that 'of course he knew about *tuc tucs*' because he was intelligent human being? Or is it possible that the only problem that existed was an overly liberal sensitivity which was always illusory?

Saturday 3rd September

An American couple has just arrived, as hurricane-ravaged New Orleans still lies underwater and devastated.

'We live in Mississippi about a hundred miles inland [from New Orleans] but since the hurricane struck we haven't had any electricity at all. Still now, all these days on, no electricity at all and we're in another State. Glad to be in England and escape it all for a few weeks.'

'There's been a lot media coverage over here but I guess you wouldn't have seen much with no electricity.'

'We ain't seen anything. Couldn't believe the TV when we arrived here. It's pretty bad. There are a lot of people angry on the ground back home. And that's Mississippi. Just as well Bush's second term is not up for re-election now because no way would he get in. We got a lot of other crazy folks as well though who don't think it's been such a bad thing. Saying New Orleans has got "god's revenge" for being such an "immoral city." Quite a few religious folks think New Orleans is too loose in its ways.'

Amazing, just as hundreds of thousands of your fellow citizens are facing an apocalyptic breakdown that Hollywood would struggle to conjure up, some are celebrating other people's misery. 'Love thy neighbour' but only if as pious and sanctimonious as you are.

Sunday 4th September

Serviced the American couple's room this morning and realised they only had one towel. It had been set up for a single occupancy before and I had forgotten to change it. They never mentioned it to us. Perhaps they are still living in 'state of emergency' conditions and expect rations to be the norm? Or maybe just because they are in Europe and have lower expectations of service compared to the States - a whole towel each rather than sharing one being the norm there? We do have electricity here though so they should be grateful at least for that. Hope they are not sinners, however, otherwise the electricity will have to be cut off.

Monday 5th September

Two journalists checked-in today before the woman flies out early tomorrow to New Orleans (via Houston) to cover the aftermath of the floods for the BBC. Their room is on the top floor and I gave them a hand up carrying some heavy suitcases and large camera equipment. They were supposed to be going to a wedding together instead tomorrow and the woman was distinctly unhappy about missing it despite my over-enthusiasm and excitement for her job assignment. Fair enough maybe - flying out alone to a dangerous disaster zone at minimal notice or going to your friend's wedding with your boyfriend - which would you prefer?

Tuesday 6th September

People who speak out loud in their sleep must constantly run the risk of their inner thoughts and subconscious being unwittingly shared, not always (if ever?) in the most desirable fashion.

'I asked him [nodding her head towards her husband] whether he was dreaming about me last night,' a woman guest told me today in a good natured tone although perhaps with a slight underlying touch of indignation.

'He said "yes,"' she continued to explain with a laugh, 'obviously thinking it would be a good thing to be dreaming about the wife. So I then asked why he also said out loud in his sleep, "stop making me feel guilty all the time you fucking bitch."'

The husband just stayed sheepishly quiet as the story was relayed, probably not too amused really to have his sleep talk shared with a stranger - probably wished he had never shared it with his wife either.

Wednesday 7th September

The party political conference season in September provides B&Bs/hotels in Brighton with probably the best trading week of the year. Normally one of the main political parties and the TUC choose Brighton as the destination for their annual conference. This not only ensures full occupancy but also enables a five night minimum stay policy to operate (the average stay for a delegate) which is much less arduous in terms of the number of check-in's/room changes etc. Additionally, many of the delegates are single person bookings despite a double room being taken and paid for (on expenses usually.)

Given the extremely high demand for conference week, rooms are normally fully booked over six months in advance. This is fine, of course, except when there is a cancellation a few days before arrival and large losses occur because the rooms cannot be re-let for five days at such short notice. To prevent these losses it is standard policy to ask for full payment twenty-one days in advance of the booking commencing. Most people are fully understanding of this requirement. However, some people can be extremely obnoxious.

Labour is here this year which means a particularly busy time because a party in government attracts a lot more media/lobby interest. All of our reservations have been paid ahead apart from one made by a local party branch in Devon. The couple due to stay have not replied to emails about payment/arrival details so today I gave them a phone call.

'Hello, I was just phoning to clarify an accommodation booking you have for the Labour Party Conference.'

'Oh not you again,' was the immediate response in an extremely hostile tone. 'Why don't you stop pestering us with your stupid payment system? We'll never book with you again in the future.'

'Excuse me. We've only sent two previous emails and are only politely asking for payment as arranged when the booking was made.'

'What a load of rubbish. We'll see you when we arrive and you can have a cheque then. Goodbye and don't pester us again,' was the reply, followed by the phone being slammed down.

Why on earth would we welcome these people into our home in a few weeks? Do they really expect us to still offer our hospitality (and leaving aside the fact that we do not even accept cheques as payments)? Following this I phoned the constituency chairman who had initially made the reservation and informed that the booking would be cancelled.

'It doesn't surprise me at all. I've had quite a few run-ins myself with those two. I was against them being chosen to represent us in the first place. Apologies for their behaviour and I don't blame you for cancelling the booking,' he told me.

This, of course, made me feel a bit better. I just hope that 'the couple' are unable to find anywhere else to stay at such short notice.

Thursday 8th September

How many artists, writers, musicians etc. create more out of vanity than any great intrinsic love for what they do? Images of future wealth and admiration being the great underlying driving force rather than a simple personal sense of achievement or enjoyment. And does it matter? Is creative endeavour more 'pure' if it lacks any ego sub-currents? Perhaps such questions only arise here because there is nothing interesting today for the diary and the struggling mind instead finds it easier to wander off into narcissistic fantasies? Surely that perfect Zen plateau where the ego has been transcended is not really true anyhow - money and smug success seems to have made plenty of others very happy.

Friday 9th September

'We're here to escape the kids for a few days,' a couple announced yesterday on arrival, with the now familiar line.

This morning at breakfast the couple were in a very jovial mood, talking and laughing a lot with each other.

'So have you been missing the kids?' I questioned.

'Nope,' they both replied instantly. 'Not at all really.'

'We just phoned home actually,' they continued, 'to remind the babysitter where the spare bed sheets are. One of our children has developed a delightful habit of swallowing bathwater every night and then wetting the bed.'

Not surprised they're glad for a break.

Saturday 10th September

Talking with some easygoing guests from Northern Ireland, the previous story of whether 'you are a Catty or a Protty?' came up in conversation (after they had informed me they were not personally religious.) Apparently there is a joke in Northern Ireland which responds to such a circumstance - 'but are you a Protestant atheist or a Catholic atheist?'

Sunday 11ᵗʰ September

A woman left behind her handbag at breakfast this morning which I noticed just as she left the dining room with her husband.

'Excuse me, is this you bag?'

'Oh Richard, look, you've forgotten your bag,' the woman said jokingly.

'Don't be so silly,' the man quickly replied, looking very embarrassed and agitated, before earnestly adding. 'I'm sorry, my wife is just being foolish. The bag is hers, honestly, not mine.'

Monday 12ᵗʰ September

Not suffering fools gladly is not the most endearing personality trait, but tolerance can often be a struggle - particularly when strangers are due to stay at your house and wind you up completely before they have even arrived.

'Hello. We have a booking with you today but forgot to bring your address. What's the name of the B&B as well and how do we find you?' someone asked, speaking on their mobile phone in the car.

'Yes, we're very easy to find,' I replied after reiterating our name and address, 'just turn left at the round-about in front of the Pier as you are driving towards the seafront, and we are five streets along on the left. Literally a few seconds drive from the pier.'

'Ok, we'll see you soon.'

Fifteen minutes later.

'Hello, it's me again. We can't seem to find your street. We're up at the Marina [a mile and a half past the pier roundabout]. Is it anywhere near here?'

'Well no, as I said before, we are just near the pier so you will need to come back into the centre. We will be five streets *back* from the pier roundabout as you drive from the Marina.'

Fifteen minutes later.

'We still can't find you. We've just gone past the Grand Hotel. Are you close to that? And what's the name of your street again?'

'No, the Grand Hotel is a mile in the *other* direction. We're right next to the functioning pier, it's impossible to miss on the seafront. We are no more than fifty metres from the pier roundabout in the direction of the marina. If you go any further you have gone too far.'

'Well, they're not very clear directions really. Can you not explain a bit more precisely because we've been looking for your street for ages now. We're getting fed up with it.'

Aaargh! Please do not find us. We do not want you to stay. There is only one seafront road. One pier roundabout. And we are five streets from that roundabout. How much more precise can you be?

Twenty minutes later we got another call.

'We think we have found the turning but whereabouts are you in the street?'

'Well our street is only about fifty metres long so you should be able to see our blue sign clearly. Hold on a second I'll look out the window.'

As I pulled the net back in the lounge I immediately saw a car outside with two gormless faces looking around in a confused fashion.

'Don't worry. I think I can see you.'

Tuesday 13th September

Quite often you have guests stay and do not get the chance to strike up any proper conversation. The same as meeting people in general life, it can make you think; 'did that person have some interesting story to tell that I've missed out on?' Of course, whenever you do hear or experience anything different, afterwards you are always grateful that such circumstances arose. This morning, despite not feeling in a particularly sociable mood, I decided to make some polite chat with a single man dressed in a casual suit staying only for one night.

'Were you in town for anything particular,' I asked the man at breakfast.

'Yes, I was giving a presentation at Sussex University last night.'

'Oh right, are you in academia then?'

'No, actually, I'm a film director. I've just finished my first feature length production this year. It's based on factual work which the University helped research. I gave a full preview film screening for them and then a question and answer session afterwards.'

After speaking a bit more I realised the film was on nationwide release and only two days previous had been featured on BBC2's *Culture Show*. How many other interesting guests have passed anonymously through the

B&B because I've been too antisocial to strike up basic pleasantries?

Wednesday 14th September

A young man, wearing a dirty vest and with a strong smell of cigarettes, knocked on the door earlier.

'I'm looking for a room,' he grunted.

'Sorry but we are fully booked,' I replied, the in-built hotelier trouble radar flashing strongly.

Later on in the day I was outside talking to the new neighbour when the same man stumbled out of their B&B now smelling strongly of both drink and cigarettes.

'Bet you're **fucking** glad I'm not staying in your house,' he immediately shouted right in my face before swaggering off like Liam Gallagher after a bottle of whiskey.

The neighbour, standing right next to me but completely ignored by his new guest in this uplifting greeting, looked mortified. It seems all hoteliers have to be baptised with a few bad guest experiences before the 'radar' becomes a bit more sensitive.

Thursday 15th September

In contrast to the frequent advice often received about 'doing something more useful with your life' it is always nice to have a reminder that leaving academia may not have been such a bad thing after all. The guests at break-fast this morning were probably disturbed by laughter from the kitchen as I read an article by Charlie Brooker, the newspaper columnist, which read; 'the single most important function of post-modernism is to give medium-wave intellectuals a clever-sounding phrase to masturbate with while the rest of us get on with our lives and ignore them.'

It took me years of hard study, being blinded with 'scientific' quotes from obscure and complicated sources, before realising that post-modernism is no more than a couple of thousand scholars worldwide, building whole careers debating semantics along a range not much bigger than a gnat's penis. All very well philosophising the abstract but it does not help much for any practical basis. Probably sounds more romantic, though, to call yourself a philosopher rather than be a boring policy wonk working out practical policy initiatives.

Friday 16th September

Listening to a mum talk overbearingly towards her twelve year old daughter at breakfast this morning it suddenly struck me that the joys of parenting could perhaps be the wonderful experience of moulding and manipulating another human being into a clone of yourself. Oops sorry. I mean a wonderful experience of bringing up a child to be an independent, free-thinking, intelligent individual.

Saturday 17th September

Radio Four on a Saturday morning does it again! Everybody in the middle of enjoying their breakfast when a ten minute segment comes on about poo being picked up from pavements by dog owners. Bon Appétit!

Sunday 18th September

The seafront drive was closed off today for speed trials of classic cars. All sorts of vehicles of all ages took their turns to individually race against the clock down towards the Marina. The upper sea road was absolutely packed as well with spectators looking down on proceedings and there was an informative but light-hearted commentary through a loud speaker system. Can understand now why the phone has been ringing so much for this weekend - the city is heaving. So much so in fact that the answer phone was needed to escape the constant ringing – allowed us to join the crowds as well.

Monday 19th September

A young foreign girl knocked on the door today inquiring about a job.

'Are you looking for a staff,' she said slowly with a heavy accent.

'I'm sorry, we do not have any job vacancies available,' I replied, resisting the urge to say yes and making a feeble joke about also requiring some robes and a long white beard.

Tuesday 20th September

In a rather morbid mood today, which perhaps befits a man entering early middle age, I was sitting philosophising the shortness of life (although a weird numbers geek may be a more apt description, as I was conceptualising the time left approximately in my life in terms of days rather than years.) Given reasonable luck another forty years should be left which equates to about fifteen thousand days. Fifteen thousand days! That's nothing surely? Days go by in seconds don't they? I can almost hear the clock ticking down to the inevitable. This could be why time is supposed to go quicker as you get older, because time is not wasted dwelling on that ticking clock when you are young - too busy just living instead.

Wednesday 21st September

Although in not such a morbid mood, the geeky conceptualisation of numbers and time are still with me. This afternoon, looking up at the sky whilst lying on the beach, I recalled reading recently that it is only a hundred miles between the Earth's surface and the outer atmosphere. Blimey! If you got into the car and was able to drive vertically up you could be in space in less than an hour. Space does not seem so far away when you view it in those terms. It makes you realise though that the air we breathe and chuck so much pollution into is such a thin little crust.

Thursday 22nd September

Notwithstanding many B&B's and hotels now getting their act together in terms of modern style and service it is apparent that quite a few *Fawlty Towers* type establishments remain. Unfortunately it is also evident that London is a particular hotspot of accommodation

SCOTT BARFIELD

'nightmares' judging by the frequent tales of our guests who arrive disappointed after staying in the capital.

'It's so nice to be in your lovely house. Our hotel in London was so awful. Everything is like paradise here in comparison,' a Dutch couple told us today, hopefully not being complimentary only because we represented *better than awful*.

'Your breakfast was really great as well. We had a buffet breakfast in London but there were only four cups available for fourteen guests. The waitress told us they were "the only ones" and to "wait for other guests to finish and then quickly grab the cups before anyone else does."'

Virtually impossible as well to get any B&B/hotel room in London for less than a £100 a night.

Friday 23rd September

Another religious conference has just taken place and an additional anecdotal observation which, may or may not have any scientific credence, is that Christian guests always seem to be meat eaters. It's so common for nearly all Christian guests to order the full cooked breakfast that we now always prepare adequate bacon in advance because we know it will all get used up. Perhaps it has something to do with the Christian stewardship tradition whereby god entrusted humans, at the apex of his creation, to legitimately use animals for their own means. For the purpose of balance though I have just found out on Wikipedia that a Christian Vegetarian Society (CVS) does exist thus proving that some Christians are not meat eaters. However, as there are only two thousand members of the CVS out of a total Christian population of over a billion people, maybe the meat eating correlation is still valid after all?

Saturday 24th September

There can't be many jobs where you get to talk to Germans about Hitler over breakfast?

'Have you been enjoying Brighton?' I asked a young German couple in the dining room this morning.

'Oh yes. It is a very beautiful city. Yesterday though we went to the cinema in the daytime because it was raining so much. The film wasn't very good but we like watching English-speaking films in their original language because in Germany they are always dubbed.'

'When foreign films are shown in England they normally come with subtitles,' I told them. 'We saw a German film actually the other week - *The Lives of Others* - it was very good.'

'Yes, that film was very successful in Germany but some people did not think it was very accurate to the Stasi. We are from Berlin and work just near where the end scenes were filmed.'

'We did see *Downfall* also not too long ago and really enjoyed that as well.'

'Oh no,' was the reply with screwed up faces aghast. 'We thought that film was *very wrong*. It should not be allowed to dramatise Hitler. Especially the way it showed him with a soft, caring side towards the German children. It is *very wrong* to humanise him. They should-n't let it happen. People should only learn about Hitler through documentaries.'

SCOTT BARFIELD

By coincidence there had been a documentary on television a couple of days ago that traced a long history of comedy sketches in the UK, both TV and film, involving Hitler over the last seventy years. From the outset we have had a culture of turning Hitler into a comedy caricature, including active government policy propaganda during the war to boost morale ('Hitler has only got one ball ...') Obviously with our history and perspective we are less sensitive than the Germans to dramatising Hitler. Enjoyable and interesting breakfast conversation though - talking to German guests about the Stasi and Hitler - who says we should never 'mention the war?'

Sunday 25th September

After an extremely hectic day today, running around sorting out numerous problems, guests probably were looking at me as some sort of *Basil Fawlty* type character. Inevitable really for comparisons to be made, especially when tired and stressed, and encountering the same sort of 'hotel' dramas. At least, however, I still managed to have another decent chat with the Germans at breakfast without any difficulties.

Monday 26th September

It was the turn of a VW Beatle rally to pack out the city for this weekend. Fascinating how a particular product brand can attract such devotion and almost instigate a whole lifestyle movement among its followers. Who said brands were a negative invention?

Tuesday 27th September

A family from mainland China - a mum, dad, son and aunt - are staying for a few days whilst visiting another son who is studying here in Brighton. There was much noisy commotion in Chinese at breakfast this morning as they seated themselves, which led me to discover five people seated around a table with only four places. The son the family is visiting had invited himself to breakfast without any advanced warning and already taken a chair and the place settings from another table and squeezed them onto where they were all sitting.

'Good morning, are you expecting breakfast for five people this morning?'

'Yes, five people, breakfast.'

'We only normally cater for the guests staying, especially without any time to prepare for extras in advance. And only four breakfasts have been paid for.'

'No, it's ok. We will pay for another breakfast. We give you a few pounds and you give five breakfasts.'

'Ok, as we are not full today we can do that for you.'

'Alright, five full breakfasts. We all want full breakfast.'

Wednesday 28th September

For the third morning in a row there are numerous cigarette butts and takeaway litter right outside our step and as I'm clearing it up some idiot walks past me and spits on the pavement.

'Thank you,' I shout, becoming consumed with fantasies of all these people being rounded up and put on an island somewhere. Then they can all sit around in their own litter, smoking and spitting at each other.

Thursday 29th September

A gay male couple who like to wear make-up is fine but, as with anyone, we prefer the make-up to be removed by other means than our pillowcases. Furthermore, switching all four top pillowcases with the four under pillowcases is not going to prevent us finding large black stains smothered everywhere. We do not leave bedding unwashed for new guests if there are no obvious outer marks left previously!

Friday 30th September

If confused about the difference between a hotel and a B&B/guest house, let me give some insight - or at least in relation to Brighton anyhow. The vast majority of the six-twelve bedroom 'hotels' are absolutely no different from a B&B or guest house. All such establishments are normally period Georgian/Victorian properties; run by couples who live on site but not with a twenty-four hour reception desk; do not provide lifts even though four/five storey buildings are the norm; and serve a similar breakfast choice over a relatively limited time period in the mornings. So if tempted by a small 'hotel' in the expectation of some greater service level or prestige, the truth is the premium charge will not really buy anything extra. Incidentally, we could be biased as we do actually call ourselves a 'guest house' – but the facts are still true, honest.

OCTOBER

Oh yes, the national star

Saturday 1St October

An English music producer has booked two rooms for single occupancy for a few days whilst helping record a new album in a Brighton studio by a Pakistani 'pop' superstar. Not being too up-to-date with Pakistan's music scene I must confess to not recognising even the name of the said superstar, let alone being overwhelmed with adulation and emotion when first meeting him in the flesh - and despite the smooth tailoring, gleaming smile and designer sunglasses.

'He's really big back in Asia,' the English producer informed me later. 'Plays to tens of thousands. He was even recognised a few times here earlier just as we were walking around town.'

Intrigued, a short google search later revealed our new guest to indeed be a multi-million selling household name in Pakistan and India. And looking through a good variety of *YouTube* clips it was quite fascinating to see our guest appear in music videos, on TV shows and award ceremonies. A real eye opener when so many representations of Muslim societies are steadfast in the 'clash of the civilizations' category. Perhaps our cultures are not so different after all - it seems the whole world now likes pop music, dancing, and poster boys/girls. Phew.

Sunday 2nd October

Our pop superstar, in the dining room this morning, was singing out loud on his mobile phone to his young daughter back in Pakistan. Not sure what the other guests at breakfast made of the song (lasting three to four minutes) but we personally liked it - a nice change anyway to the news on the *Today* programme.

'I had a look at your website. It seems you're reasonably well known back in Pakistan,' I later said in a deliberately understated way to try and avoid being sycophantic.

'Oh yes. I'm the national star.'

Maybe globalisation has yet to take place for irony or any false sense of modesty?

Monday 3rd October

Our pop superstar friend, just before departing today, insisted on having photos taken with Helen and me outside the B&B. After about ten minutes, at his request, we had covered nearly every combination of standing positions and different angles and multiple shots to make sure he would have memories of us forever. Perhaps he took me too seriously when he heard the book I had (not even yet) written had made us and our B&B the nation's favourite?

Tuesday 4th October

There is a certain breed of straight, English couples (usually over fifty years old) who occupy a distinctive and different cultural landscape and who probably shouldn't visit Brighton, or at least not stay in Kemp Town.

'Certainly very cosmopolitan round here isn't? Cor. We couldn't believe it last night. We were in a bar just round the corner and there was a transvestite in there and another guy dressed all in leathers. We only wanted a quiet drink. We didn't realise it was a gay bar,' a man said earlier whilst shaking his head disapprovingly.

'Yes, the city certainly has a few characters. You can normally tell a lot of the gay places round here because they have the Rainbow flag outside.'

'Well, I'm just not used to that sort of thing. We don't have any gays back where I'm from. They were all ok, I guess, didn't cause us any bother at all.'

'Oh well, we're leaving here tomorrow, so you won't have to put up with it much longer,' his wife then added.

'You shouldn't worry too much anyway about being "bothered" around here,' I said. 'You're probably not their type.'

Wednesday 5th October

'Have you been married long?' asked a single man who we knew was a Christian because a copy of the New Testament has been on his bedside cabinet for the last few days.

'We're not married actually,' I told him directly back, more than happy that 'living in sin' was a retrograde concept for the 21st century.

'Oh really,' he responded sincerely with a look of shock and disapproval. 'Well I hope not too far into the future you will make an honest woman of Helen.'

Surely being a sanctimonious busy-body is a bit out of date now as well?

Thursday 6th October

Electricity (or the ability to harness it at least) must be one of the greatest human inventions of all time. That's my conclusion anyway after an eerie few hours today when visions of a post apocalyptic world were brought close to mind. Ten minutes after finishing breakfast all the lights suddenly went out, the radio went off and every appliance cut out as well. Almost immediately we had the guests come down to tell us there was no power in the rooms, including one person in a towel who was midway through an (electric) shower. Normally I would just check the fuse box for any that had tripped, but none had and there was absolutely no power anywhere in the house. No lights, telephone, computer, internet, radio, television, showers, clocks, vacuum cleaner, dishwasher, washing machine, tumble dryer, iron, oven, microwave, fridge, freezer - even the toaster wouldn't work! Ok, in many parts of the world life still continues without electricity (and toast), but we're not used to it here and hotel guests paying good money to be pampered are especially not happy to go back-to-basics.

Looking outside I could hear no alarms going off, which you would expect with a general power cut, and all our neighbours still had their lights on and were continuing with normal life. Great. It was just our building that was experiencing the quiet impotence of life without any mod cons. Luckily the mobile phone was still working and the electricity board were able to come and fix our electricity withdrawal symptoms by replacing the mains fuse into the house. This took three hours though so we all had some time (or I did anyway) to reflect on how life would be in a world without electricity. Quite nice in some ways to just sit in silence with no phone to answer, emails to check, or vacuuming to do. The guy who had to rinse the shampoo out of his hair with cold water in the sink did not seem so philosophically enthralled however.

Friday 7ᵗʰ October

'Did you enjoy your night out?' I asked two women who had booked in yesterday and were unenthusiastically attending the Hen party of a work colleague (all the others staying elsewhere thankfully).

'Oh it was awful,' they responded instantly in unison.

'We ended up sneaking off as soon as we could get away without anyone spotting us,' one of them continued. 'First, though, we had to endure an absolutely hideous male strip show at this really tacky venue on the edge of town where loads of other Hen groups were also booked in. It was a nightmare.'

'We've just been saying to each other actually,' said the other woman, 'that we think a different word needs to be invented for those who want to have a pre-wedding get together in a civilised way. "Hen" and "Stag" parties seem to only describe a really ghastly night.'

'We've been dreading this weekend for ages,' her friend carried on. 'Spent a fortune to dress up horribly, go to an awful club, and watch the bride-to-be get horrendously drunk whilst carrying a giant inflatable willy and having a "last snog" with some other drunk creep.'

Saturday 8ᵗʰ October

'Yeah mate. Yooz got any rooms for next weekend.'

'What kind of rooms are you looking for?'

'There's about twenty-five of uz. Wiz don't mind sharing three/four to a room. Whatever yooz can do.'

'I'm sorry but we only have rooms for a maximum of two people and we do not accommodate large groups either.'

'Oh yeah mate. Wot's the problem with large groups then?'

'Because we generally find it too rowdy and people also tend to drink too much.'

'Oh yeah. Well what if all of uz book separate then?'

'Well it would still be a large group staying with us so we would not accept any of the bookings.'

'Well you're not going to know, are yer mate?'

'Why cause unnecessary bother for yourselves and us and just go to a larger hotel where groups are welcome?'

'Don't care mate, really, what you fink. Weez all gonna stay at your place.'

At which point I hang up.

Sunday 9ᵗʰ October

'Happy birthday,' I said to a woman as she entered the dining room, remembering her reason for staying with us. 'Your day to be treated and spoilt then?'

'Well, not too spoilt at the moment,' she replied with raised eyebrows and a shrug of the head. 'He's too lazy [her partner] to get out of bed and told me to come to breakfast by myself!'

Evidently 'Mr Amours' are quite common.

Monday 10th October

Brighton's comedy festival is on at the moment for three weeks which always brings a few extra guests seeing the various different shows. Similar to people staying when going to a music concert it can be interesting to match up different personalities with their music/comedy tastes - well, interesting at least for us nosy, observational and judgemental types with nothing much better to do.

Is it important for people - if they are going to be friends/lovers - to share similar music/comedy/cultural tastes? Opposite attraction is surely just a myth when most people actually pair off to someone with a close background and interests. Anyhow, the fact that two new guests have a diametrically different sense of humour to my own is not a problem - especially as both are not my type.

'Are you in town for any particular reason?'

'Yes, actually, we have tickets to see *Ross Noble* tonight at the Brighton Dome.'

'Oh right, that should be good,' I enthusiastically (rep) lied, not being a huge fan.

'We were supposed to go to the Dome tomorrow to see *Mitchell and Webb*,' I added. 'Couldn't stand their new sketch show though so cancelled.'

'Oh. We really loved their TV series. In fact we got tickets to see them as well.'

No big deal. B&B owners and their guests can amicably agree to disagree - they were probably not interested in me either as a friend or lover.

Tuesday 11th October

Traffic wardens really do ask for a bad reputation in certain circumstances. A couple approached me today to query why they had received a £60 parking ticket when the 'hotel guest' voucher had been scratched out correctly. As I double-checked their vehicle which was parked right outside the B&B a traffic warden was walking past.

'Hello. My guests here have received a ticket. As far as I can see it has all been filled out properly? Has there been a mistake?' I asked politely.

'The voucher has been placed on the driver's side of the vehicle. It clearly states on the back on the back of the voucher that it must be displayed on the nearside to the kerb. That's why a ticket has been issued.'

A £60 fine all because the small print in the 'rules' say that a traffic warden cannot stretch his irritating neck an extra few inches to see marginally further along the dashboard.

Wednesday 12th October

House prices are starting to fall so inevitably we are all now bombarded with messages of doom and gloom and disaster.

'Has the credit crunch affected business much,' has been a typical question that some guests have asked in making conversation recently.

House prices are only going back to where they were two years ago however so it's only very recent buyers that have lost out. All others still have previous windfall gains under their belts and the millions not yet on the ladder (or wanting to move up the ladder) are going to be better off from price falls. It's funny how lower prices are 'good news' for everything else we buy, but not houses, the single biggest purchase most of us ever make in our lives?

Thursday 13th October

'We've really enjoyed our few days here, thank you,' a young couple told us whilst checking out.

'We stayed at this really weird B&B last time we were in Brighton,' they continued. 'The owner cornered us in the hallway and insisted we sit in their living room with them and watch a home movie!'

'Sounds a bit dodgy,' I said.

'Well it wasn't quite a home movie in the really dodgy sense but it was still bad enough. It was from the owner's holiday in Greece where there was a *hilarious* Roy "Chubby" Brown impersonator. We had to sit through the whole lot. We couldn't escape.'

'Well I've got some photos of my last trip to Italy if you want to have a look,' I offered in response but they declined.

Friday 14th October

Found bits of kebab meat on the hallway carpet as I opened up this morning. Then, surveying around a bit more, I discovered a couple of chillies (red and green) on the stairs, along with some soggy pieces of lettuce a bit further up. Strange coincidence again that such things only seem to occur when guests are staying that you were already unsure about? Being a B&B owner is definitely good for developing powers of intuition.

Saturday 15th October

Losing all your money and passports at the start of a long holiday abroad is not most people's idea of fun. A cheerful young couple from New Zealand arrived after spending five nights in London at the beginning of a six week tour of Britain. Ten minutes after checking in, however, the woman knocked back on the door looking flustered.

'Sorry to bother you but we need help. My boyfriend left our money belt in the hotel room in London. Both our passports and thousands in cash were in the belt. Could you look up the number of the hotel for us because we don't have it?'

Luckily I quickly found the number on the internet and the hotel had already discovered the 'forgotten' money belt intact. An immediate return trip to London and not yet retrieving lost money and passports would have left many people still feeling stressed and agitated. This Kiwi couple, however, resumed their previous cheerfulness straightaway.

'Oh well. These things happen. We'll still get to see Brighton hopefully, just a bit later then originally planned.'

Sunday 16th October

Generally speaking, when the guests start conversations with each other in the dining room, it adds pleasantly to the general ambience of the B&B - and often provides some amusing banter to earwig. The last few days we have had a down-to-earth English couple in their sixties talking about all sorts with a friendly young Spanish couple.

'We went to the theatre last night,' the older English man said at breakfast today. 'We saw *The Rocky Horror Show*. Have you ever heard of it?'

'No. No. We do not know that. Is it a good play?' the Spaniards replied.

'Well I'm not sure you can exactly call it a play,' the English man continued laughing loudly. 'Normally you don't get men in the audience dressed in stockings, suspenders and high heels when you go to the theatre.'

'It sounds very strange,' the Spaniards responded, obviously completely bewildered to what sort of conversation was occurring.

'Don't get me too wrong. I wasn't dressed like that myself. And it's the first time as well I've ever been to a men's toilet and stood next to a six foot six transvestite! Honestly, you should go and see it. The show is very famous in England.'

'Ok, maybe.'

'He did really wear stockings and suspenders,' I announced at this point as I entered the dining room. 'I saw him leaving the house last night all dressed up.'

We all laughed at this point but the Spaniards a bit more apprehensively.

Monday 17th October

A posh and plummily spoken mum arrived today with her nine year old son who was wearing schoolboy shorts and a baseball cap.

'Do I look like a chav with this baseball cap on,' the boy said haughtily to me, much to the embarrassment of his mother. 'I look like I'm a chav, don't I?'

Presumably the boy had previously got a laugh from pretending to be obviously 'beneath' himself. The joke, however, may have worked better if his affectedly rich pronunciation did not make the word sound more like 'charve.'

Tuesday 18th October

Our engineer came today to replete our fire extinguisher which 'had' or 'had not' been previously let off.

'Last week I was at a B&B,' he told us, 'where the guests had smoked underneath the duvet covers to avoid setting the smoke alarm off. The sheets and mattress were left stinking of smoke and full of cigarette burns.'

That's a new one. Perhaps all our previous guests who have merely smoked out of the window have not thought of this ingenious method to try and avoid smoke detection?

Wednesday 19th October

There is never a truer saying than 'you can't please all of the people all of the time.' And running a B&B, or any other customer-orientated business, it is wise to become slightly de-sensitive to the vagaries of people's personalities.

Two days ago we had a somewhat scathing review left online from a couple who were permanently miserable for their entire stay (despite our very best host endeavours) and then another couple leave today, staying in exactly the same room, be completely opposite in overgushing about how 'wonderful and marvellous everything has been.' How can two near identical experiences be perceived so differently? The truth probably relates to the fact that a certain percentage of people are just natural miserable pessimists who go constantly through life determined to only see the negatives - hey Mr Wells from Bury St Edmunds?

Thursday 20th October

Incidentally, anyone planning on a visit to Brighton who does not enjoy the following - close proximity to a large variety of restaurants, pubs, shops, theatres, live music, other people generally; historic architecture (especially Regency sash windows instead of white PVC double glazing); the beach; the sea; or B&B's where a younger female (who doesn't particularly like golf) may show you up to your room and be in charge - please be warned, it may not be to your liking.

Friday 21st October

'I wanna book a triple room.'

'Sorry but we no longer have any triple rooms, only doubles and twins.'

'Yeh, but there *iz* three of us.'

'Well you would need two rooms then.'

'Why *iz* that?'

'Because our rooms only accommodate a maximum of two people.'

'We'll just have a twin room then and one of *uz* will sleep on the floor.'

'Well, like I've just said, you can't do that.'

'Why not?'

'Because our rooms only hold two people.'

'Ok, whatever. We'll just book one twin room for tonight.'

'Sorry we're fully booked anyway [and always will be].'

Saturday 22nd October

Is a cold sore on your nose a valid excuse for being late and, even if it is, would you actually want to use it anyhow? Our normal latest check-in time is 8pm unless guests specifically arrange later. This evening we received a phone call at 8.30pm from a woman who was running behind schedule.

'Sorry about this. I'm in Crawley at the moment so will definitely arrive a bit late. I'm also waiting for my PA to get back to me with advice from NHS Direct because I have a cold sore on my nose.'

'Ok, thanks for letting us know where you are, and hopefully we will see you soon,' I replied whilst slightly bemused at the unexpected additional medical information.

It was less amusing, however, when there was still no sign of the woman two hours later and no response either from her mobile phone. Eventually, though, at 11pm the doorbell went.

'Hi there. Sorry for being so late. I had to wait for my PA to get back to me and then had to drive all round Crawley to find a late night chemist,' a woman in her late thirties, dressed in a business suit, told me as I opened the door.

Although annoyed at the lateness, maybe such an excuse is legitimate because who in their right mind would want to make up this alibi? In fact, it was true, because I stared long and hard at her nose to make sure there was a cold sore there.

Sunday 23rd October

Michel, the French rocker, is back only this time with his girlfriend.

'What's your plans for today,' I asked them.

'We are both going to get another tattoo done. We always get new tattoos every time we visit Brighton. I go to this place I found years ago when I used to live here - he's the best.'

'Oh right. Have you already decided what kind of tattoo to have done?'

'Oh yes. We are going to have each other's names tattooed on our arms in "Elvish" - you know, the Elf language from the *Lord of the Rings*.'

Later on in the evening they showed me their new body artwork. Looked alright but I cannot read Elvish so couldn't tell whether their names were spelt correctly or not?

Monday 24th October

The Today programme did a long piece on the night-mare that Iraq has turned into, detailing such facts as half of Baghdad residents having had a family member murdered in the last four years, economic collapse, ethnic cleansing, growing religious extremism etc and then moved immediately on to an upbeat feature about a new list detailing "the most tranquil places to live in Britain." No sense of irony or acknowledgement of the juxtaposition - 'ah, enough of all that depressing stuff about how shit things are in Iraq, lets focus instead on the many wonderful tranquil places that exist in our green and pleasant land.'

Tuesday 25th October

Being a male living in Kemp Town you get to experience a little of what females the world over must face on a regular basis - the ogling, overtly sexual, eyes of men. Now don't get me wrong, I'm not trying to put special tickets on myself, all would probably notice the same with a bit of Gaydar tuning - Quasimodo would so long as he still had a dick. But walking down St James's Street it is noticeable that gay men often try to catch the eye and, equally indiscreetly, an evident glance to survey the male 'goods' below - perhaps in the same way numerous straight men find it difficult to not stare down at female cleavage. Given that most straight men have probably never experienced (or noticed) such direct sexual gawping in any form, would their own salivating ogling become more circumspect if they realised exactly how it came across?

Wednesday 26th October

Another social observation from living in Kemp Town is that toilet etiquette in gay bars can be a bit different. Last night we met up with a few of the neighbours for a 'B&B owners get together' and ended up being in a gay bar – not my usual hang out, but a convenient place round the corner to have a drink and a chat. Whilst using the urinal in the toilet, however, another man came in and started using the adjacent urinal despite the fact that another six along were all empty.

'Where do you come from then, darling?'

Elsewhere in the male toilets of the country, of course, there is an unwritten law that states you never go next to someone if there are other empty urinals and, never, do you make any 'polite' conversation with strangers.

Thursday 27th October

Running a B&B together as a couple you should be aware, and able to cope with the fact, that you can literally spend twenty four hours a day with your partner. Obviously for some romantic devils this notion could sound like domestic heavenly bliss. For others though, surely, it could be domestic hell. Luckily for Helen and me it is the former and we have never argued or even had one crossed word. In fact, compared to the average couple who work apart and only actually see each other a few hours a day, we have now (in 'normal' relationship years) been happily together for the equivalent of one hundred and twenty-five years.

Friday 28th October

Some more Christian guests staying at the moment and, once more, I am slightly envious of the fact that all of them possess a certain level of happiness that apparently emanates from belief in a higher power, a drug-like contentment perhaps - the 'opium of the masses.' What drugs though are us atheists, who also desire a state of bliss, supposed to use when we do not believe in any of that god stuff? Real opium? Or maybe just a nice glass of red wine?

Saturday 29th October

Sometimes people do say some odd things.

'Sorry but we are fully booked for that weekend,' I politely told a man with a broad Welsh accent on the phone today who was enquiring about a very busy week-end forthcoming.

'Well thanks a lot for your help then you big poo on a stick,' he responded before hanging up.

Sunday 30th October

A sporty type guy is staying from Sydney.

'I used to live in Australia actually when I was a bit younger,' I told him, just making a bit of light conversation. 'I was in Melbourne for about eighteen months.'

'Whooa, mate,' he responded, feigning a bit of shock and horror, but really with some seriousness. 'Sorry to hear that mate, it must have been tough on yer. Never tell a Sydneysider that - the two cities have never got on with each other.'

'Well, I did spend a bit of time in Sydney as well. Both places are great cities,' I truthfully replied.

'Nah, mate. Melbourne's got nothing on Sydney. We got the harbour, the weather, sports, everything's better. You should have lived in Sydney and then you would have never come back.'

Amazing how strong the territorial gene seems to linger on in human evolution - between countries, cities, neighbourhoods within cities, streets within neighbourhoods - anything divisive that people can latch on to. Maybe we need to discover life on another planet somewhere and then we can all rally round the 'home turf' of planet Earth.

Monday 31st October

'Excuse me,' a German guest summoned me during a full breakfast session this morning, 'Could you tell my wife and me what is the difference between "jam" and "marmalade?"'

'Erm, I'm not sure,' perplexed momentarily, having never given much thought to the question before. 'Does anyone else know?' I asked round the room to the other listening guests who were all English.

After an ensuing big group discussion on the subject,

which lasted a good number of riveting minutes, I returned to the somewhat bemused German guests.

'There seems to be some disagreement on the exact difference but marmalade, basically, has a more bitter taste because it is made from citrus fruits whereas normal jam would be made from other fruits such as strawberries which are sweeter.'

'Oh. That is so very interesting. In Germany we only have the one word to describe all types of jam [and marmalade.] We do not use two descriptions. Thank you very much for telling us.'

'That's ok. Thank you. Your question has prompted a lively debate for everyone at this early hour. Given us all some food for thought.'

NOVEMBER AGAIN

A full year!

Tuesday 1st November

Are there any known preliminary common behaviour patterns which potentially indicate a personality predisposed towards becoming a stalker? The reason I ask, and hopefully not to cause any alarm for any guests (past, present and future) who might be reading, is that I have developed a habit which could possibly be defined as unhealthily snooping - although hopefully just a normal sense of curiosity facilitated by modern technology?

Already I probably spend far too much time looking at Google Earth, often in conjunction with looking up estate agent property details from every corner of the world - sad, I know (but surely there are others out there?) Anyhow, given that whenever an online booking is made, full address details are given, the satellite viewing penchant has now evolved into often looking up the house and area of where the guest lives. Nothing creepy really about that is there?

Wednesday 2nd November

Another thing in relation to satellite snooping, aside from pervs from NASA zooming in live on people sunbathing naked in their back gardens, is the thought that aliens from another planet could theoretically be looking down some ultra powerful telescope at us all here on planet Earth. If NASA can now achieve clear imagery close up to a few metres, why not some ET from one of the trillions of other planets out there? For all we know the Earth right at this moment could be like some *Truman Show* reality style soap opera that the Aliens sit down to watch every night for peak time viewing?

Thursday 3ʳᵈ November

A few weeks ago a woman booked in advance from London with the same name of this year's winner of the Whitbread/Costa book award, a book which Helen had also happened to have just read. Being inquisitive, of course, we had already researched a bit further and were able to recognise her as the author when she turned up a few days ago. Not wanting to be sycophantic, or potentially make the author feel uncomfortable whilst staying here, we had not asked whether she was the writer until she checked out this morning. Maybe a bit embarrassing for us both, but authors apparently do not often get recognised, so secretly it could have been a bit flattering - even more so, perhaps, when I also told her a guest staying in the same room last week had been reading her book.

Friday 4ᵗʰ November

Is honesty always the best policy or does sometimes it just scare old ladies unnecessarily? Two Canadian women guests in their seventies are due to visit London after staying with us in Brighton.

'We're very worried about terrorism when we get to London after all those bombings. We decided we're not going anywhere near the tube at all. No way worth the risk. We'll just use the buses only to get around.'

'Well you know a bus was blown up as well in those last bombings?' I told them helpfully. The useful information, however, was not much appreciated.

Saturday 5th November

Be warned, anyone trying to book a B&B/hotel room using well known 'traveller review' sites, many unscrupulous owners *definitely* spend a lot of time posting up sparkling fake reviews. The closest we have got to manipulating the rankings was last week when my mum stayed and we asked her to post a review - after all she was still a guest of sorts. However, seeing the review listed today, perhaps we shouldn't have bothered asking. Only a four out of five rating, along with an additional few negative comments such as "parking being difficult," even though my mum actually got easily parked right outside!

'Well, I wanted to try and give some balance - otherwise they may have thought the review was a fake.'

What chance for a great review from ordinary guests when your own mum only rates you four out of five? Because the average score as well for B&Bs in the top twenty is around four and half out of five, the review actually reduced our average and knocked us a few places down in the overall rankings.

Sunday 6th November

The mass London to Brighton trip for this weekend was the turn of the veteran car rally. Not sure that all the old cars actually made it to Brighton, and most that did were put on trailers for the return journey home, but the event added some nice character to the city. On arrival, given the late autumn chill and the exposed nature of many of the cars, quite a few of the participants had a slightly frozen statuesque look about them. The kids along for the ride, enthusiastic no doubt at the beginning, were particularly struggling (fifty chilly miles on) to greet the welcoming crowds.

Monday 7th November

'Dangerous spiders on rise in Sussex,' was the headline in the local newspaper today. The downside of the mild climate this side of the South Downs is that poisonous spiders from the Black Widow family, originally stowaways in banana shipments from the Canary Islands, have managed to establish a number of thriving nests. If bitten by one of these spiders the poison apparently attacks the nervous system and has been known to induce heart attacks.

'Urgh. I'm moving back up North if the spiders get too established,' was Helen's response.

Tuesday 8th November

By sheer coincidence we had two separate couples arrive yesterday, both here to celebrate their 50th wedding anniversaries. Talking to each other in the dining room at breakfast this morning, after being introduced, it transpired also that the eldest grandchild of each couple had both just turned eighteen. Statistically very unlikely, of course, for the two couples to arrive here at the same time but that's the 'certainty of chance' for you. As we were all together in the dining room, a segment happened to come on the radio which announced that Premium Bonds and *ERNIE* were also celebrating their 50th anniversary today.

'There you go,' I said to them all. 'That's the romantic icing on the cake - both your marriages are the same age as premium bonds!'

Wednesday 9th November

We made it! One whole year as B&B owners! That's it - I am off to open the champagne, and more than likely to quickly proceed to the red wine. Good excuse as any. Summary thoughts on how the year has been will have to wait until after. Cheers …

Epilogue

Ok. Some honesty. The material that makes up this book, although all based on real events and experiences, actually occurred over a three year timeframe rather than exactly fitting in neatly to a year long diary. The truth, of course, is that daily life (including the exhilarating existence of a B&B owner) is just not so exciting on average. However, despite the elongated time to collect sufficient interesting stories, hopefully this does not detract from the main premise of the book. Additionally, the entries are chronologically listed as far as possible vis-à-vis smooth formatting, and key days/dates match up in the vast majority of cases – indeed, my life as a B&B owner did really start on Wednesday 10th November!

Notwithstanding the highlighting of some of the more unsavoury aspects of B&B owner life, it should be said also that virtually all of the real 'horror' stories took place in our first six months. Undoubtedly there are certain risks involved with the B&B lifestyle, but with experience it is possible to largely avoid these hazards. If reading this book having recently stayed with us (or in the house now) then feel privileged – you are one of the lucky ones to make it through our vigorous screening system!

Anyhow let's not dwell too much on negatives when the B&B owner lifestyle has overall been a positive experience. Yes it has been 'ever such hard work' in places with a small minority being a right pain in the backside, but mostly you meet pleasant people of all nationalities and get the flexibility and independence of being your boss. It is also impossible, in reality, to describe a uniform 'B&B experience.' Running a twelve-bedroom B&B at full effort is not the same as owning six-bedroom B&B and working it at 60% - there really isn't any law (mortgage permitting) that stops you closing off the rooms whenever you need a break.

In regards to our neighbours we have bad news to any visitor wanting to secretly (or openly?) have a look at the bondage establishment – it no longer exists. I'm sure, however, that the vegetarian, gay, male bondage scene is still happening somewhere if you do want to find it. Our argumentative neighbours on the other side, incidentally, have also moved on and the easy-going new arrivals do not appear to like either vodka binges or Queen/Meatloaf karaoke.

And the Zen? Well, surely it would be a bit paradoxical to dictate insights if the emphasis is supposed to be on personal realisation? Just hope you enjoyed sharing my little journey.